Passport's Illustr

KENYA

FROM
THOMAS
COOK

PASSPORT BOOKS
a division of *NTC Publishing Group*
Lincolnwood, Illinois USA

GW00701474

Published by Passport Books,
an imprint of NTC/Contemporary Publishing Company,
4255 W. Touhy Avenue,
Lincolnwood (Chicago), Illinois
60646–1975 U.S.A.

Written by Melissa Shales

Original photography by Paul Kenward

Edited, designed and produced by AA Publishing.
Maps © The Automobile Association 1994, 1996.

The contents of this publication are believed correct at the
time of printing. Nevertheless, the publishers cannot accept
responsibility for errors or omissions, or for changes in details
given in this guide, or for the consequences of any reliance on
the information provided by the same. Assessments of
attractions, hotels, restaurants, and so forth are based upon the
author's own experience and, therefore, descriptions given in
this guide necessarily contain an element of subjective opinion that may
not reflect the publishers' opinion or dictate a reader's own experiences
on other occasions.
**We have tried to ensure accuracy in this guide, but things do
change and we would be grateful if readers would advise us of any
inaccuracies they may encounter.**

Library of Congress Catalog Card Number: 93-84396

ISBN 0-8442-4831-2

Published by Passport Books in conjunction with AA Publishing and the
Thomas Cook Group Ltd.

Color separation: BTB Colour Reproduction, Whitchurch, Hampshire,
England

Printed by Edicoes ASA, Oporto, Portugal.

Third printing 1997.

Contents

About this Book

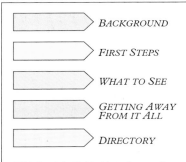

> BACKGROUND
>
> FIRST STEPS
>
> WHAT TO SEE
>
> GETTING AWAY FROM IT ALL
>
> DIRECTORY

This book is divided into five sections, identified by the above colour coding.

Background gives an introduction to the country – its history, geography, politics and culture.
First Steps offers practical advice on arriving and getting around.

Cheetahs in Samburu National Reserve

What to See is an alphabetical listing of places to visit, divided into six regions, interspersed with walks and tours.
Getting Away From it All highlights places off the beaten track where it is possible to relax and enjoy the peace and quiet.
Finally, the *Directory* provides practical information – from shopping and entertainment to children and sport, including a section on business matters. Special highly illustrated *features* on specific aspects of the country appear throughout the book.

MAPPING
The maps in this book use international country symbols:
SD Sudan. EAU Zaïre
ETH Ethiopia. SO Somalia
EAT Tanzania.

BACKGROUND

'Africa, for many travellers,
it's an object of desire, they talk of love
at first sight, seduction, awakening,
rebirth. Why Africa? Why do
Westerners like myself keep returning to
a continent to which we have no claim?'

JOHN HEMINWAY,
The Africa Passion, Channel 4 TV (1993)

Introduction

*K*enya bestrides the Equator at the cross-roads of Africa, separating the burning deserts of the north from the vast rolling plateaux of the south, its culture built by immigrants from all over Africa, the Middle East, Asia and Europe. Home to one of the world's last great reservoirs of wildlife, it has an extraordinary variety of natural habitats, from coral reefs to open grasslands and tropical forest. Its people live in thatched huts and cosmopolitan cities. Above all, it is quite spectacularly beautiful.

The vast Rift Valley, which slashes its way across the country, is now recognised as the birth place of mankind.

This is the original Garden of Eden. But as in the ancient story, paradise is not without its troubles. Kenya is struggling to survive against drought, a massive population explosion and threatened economic chaos. The very survival of the country's natural riches depends, to a large extent, on tourism. A sophisticated tourist infrastructure offers every

The great Rift Valley, a 6,000km scar across Africa, seen near Nairobi

---

❖

THOMAS COOK'S
Kenya

Thomas Cook became involved in Kenyan tourism almost as soon as the country was born, taking parties down the Nile and through the Sudan. In 1903, they were appointed official agents for the East African Railway, but most of their tours were hunting safaris centred on Nairobi. In 1935, a local manager set up the first motoring tour of East Africa, a prototype of all motoring safaris today.

❖

KENYA IN AFRICA

SUDAN ETHIOPIA
Lake Turkana
ZAÏRE UGANDA SOMALIA
Lake Victoria **KENYA**
RWANDA ■ **Nairobi**
BURUNDI
■ **Mombasa**
TANZANIA Zanzibar INDIAN OCEAN
ZAMBIA

KENYA

possibility from a lazy fortnight under the coconut palms, to high adventure out in the bush many miles from civilisation, from tiny tents to luxury hotels that rival the finest in the world. Visitors are welcomed with open arms, every effort is made to ensure their stay is never tainted by the slightest whiff of trouble, and few return home without falling deeply under the spell of this fascinating land.

History

4–2 million years ago
Excavations from the 1960s onwards by the Leakey family provide the earliest known evidence of human existence on earth suggesting the East African Rift Valley as the birthplace of mankind.

200,000–150,000BC
Acheulian Stone Age cultures living in the Rift Valley.

10,000–5,000BC
Hunter-gatherer tribes, thought to be related to the San and Khoikhoi of South Africa, living in Kenya.

2,000–1,000BC
A series of Cushite migrations south from Ethiopia and Somalia (see pages 14–15).

1,000BC
Earliest Nilotic migration south from the Nile Valley.

500BC–AD500
Earliest Bantu migration from West Africa. The Bantu migration and readjustment of tribal boundaries continues until frozen by the British in the 19th century.

2nd century AD
Diogenes and Ptolemy, two Greek geographers living in Egypt, separately visit the East African coast and write of their experiences.

650–800
Arab and Persian trading posts are set up along the coast. Many traders settle and intermarry, introducing the Islamic religion and creating the Swahili people and language.

1498–99
First contact with Europeans when the Portuguese explorer Vasco da Gama, the first westerner to sail around the Cape of Good Hope to Asia, anchors off Mombasa, then sets up a trading post at Malindi.

Early 16th century
Mombasa sacked by Francisco d'Almeida in 1505 and Nuña da Cunha in 1528. Portuguese take over as rulers.

1696–8
Portuguese settlements attacked and conquered by Omanis.

1729
Portuguese finally surrender Fort Jesus, their last toehold on the coast north of Mozambique.

1741
Mazrui governor of Mombasa declares independence from Oman.

1824
Sultan of Oman attempts to reclaim coast. The Mazrui ask for British aid and sign a treaty offering a loose British Protectorate.

1826–1837
British aid withdrawn and the Mazrui are defeated. Bey Saidi Sultan Sayyid Said moves his capital to Zanzibar.

1873
Omani-British treaty bans the export of slaves and closes all slave markets.

1888
The Imperial British East Africa Company, under Sir William Mackinnon, receives a Royal Charter.

1895
British Government declares East Africa a Protectorate, taking over direct rule and leasing a 16km stretch of coast from the Sultan of Zanzibar.

1896–1901
East African Railway (the Lunatic Line) built from Mombasa to Lake Victoria, opening up the Kenya highlands for European development. 20,000 Indians imported to build and run the railway.

1899
Nairobi founded as an inland railhead.

1907
Nairobi becomes capital of the East African Protectorate.

1920–23
The East African Protectorate becomes a Crown Colony. Soldier-settler scheme offers cheap land to British ex-service-men, leading to massive immigration.

1950–1960
Mau Mau terror campaign by Kikuyu nationalists seeking independence. Mau Mau banned in 1950. A State of Emergency declared in 1952, with many leaders arrested. In 1954, 30,000 Kikuyu detained for questioning and 20,000 imprisoned as suspected Mau Mau supporters. In total, 13,500 Africans and 100 Europeans die during the troubles.

1960
Lancaster House conference in London paves the way to independence.

1963
Kenya gains independence with Jomo Kenyatta as Prime Minister. The last Sultan of Zanzibar, Seyyid Khalifa, cedes his lands to Kenya.

1964
Kenya becomes a republic, with Kenyatta as executive president. Parliament is reduced to one house and the country effectively becomes a one-party state.

1968
A policy of Africanisation is instated. Land bought from white settlers is divided into smallholdings and given to African farmers. Large-scale emigration by nervous Asians.

1974
Kiswahili becomes the official language.

1978
Kenyatta dies and is replaced, without election, by Vice-President Moi.

1982
Moi survives an attempted Air Force coup.

1987
Kenya declared a one-party state under the Kenya African National Union.

1992
International pressure forces president Moi to hold multi-party elections. Moi holds on to power, but now faces a strong parliamentary opposition.

Half a million refugees flood across the border from war-torn Somalia.

1992–present
Some refugees remain, but many have returned home. Another general election is expected in 1997.

Politics

*K*enya is a Commonwealth Republic. It has a single house of parliament of 200 members, 188 elected by universal suffrage and 12 appointed by the president, who governs with the aid of a 33-member cabinet. Now, as at independence, the country is officially a multi-party democracy, but the road between has been rocky.

Kenyatta's rule

The 1963 elections were contested by two parties, the Kenya African National Union (KANU) and the Kenya African Democratic Union (KADU). However, both were splinters of the primarily Kikuyu Kenya African Union (KAU). In 1964, they merged again and Kenya became an unofficial one-party state. During Kenyatta's presidency, however, this state of affairs did not seem oppressive. There was a little corruption and violence, but Kenya was a glowing beacon of wealth and stability compared to many black African countries.

Moi's rule

In 1978, however, Kenyatta died and was succeeded by his vice-president, Daniel Arap Moi, a member of the Tugen tribe. From the first, criticism was silenced and after the failed Air Force coup in 1982, all opposition was stifled. In 1987, the country officially became a one-party state, the press was muzzled, and Moi's powers were increased, now including the right to sack any member of the civil service or judiciary. In the 1987 elections, voters had to line up physically behind their preferred candidate. A rising tide of corruption threatened to engulf the country.

1992

In 1992, international pressure forced Moi to hold multi-party elections with a secret ballot, monitored by international observers. Two main opposition parties, the Democratic Party and FORD, the Forum for the Restoration of Democracy were created, divided along tribal lines. The Kikuyus switched their allegiance to the DP, while FORD was largely supported by the Luo. Campaigning was based on personalities and dirt-mongering. Policies were never mentioned. Inter-tribal violence broke out, and politicians openly handed out sackfuls of money. Most people kept their heads down, agreed with everyone and some even joined all three parties. By the time of the election, the opposition was hopelessly fragmented, with seven presidential candidates. The observers refused to acknowledge the election 'free and fair', but agreed that the result could stand as there had been illegalities on all sides.

In the end, Moi and KANU stayed in power, but they now only have a narrow majority in Parliament. Most opposition followers regard this as a triumph. Under pressure from the World Bank and the international community, a half-hearted effort is being made to clean up the corruption, while white Kenyan, Richard Leakey (second son of Louis and Mary Leakey, see page 134), and his new political party, Safina, are spearheading the search for a credible opposition candidate. Few believe that President Moi will win the next election.

KENYATTA

Johnstone Kamau was born in 1892, son of a Kikuyu peasant. Educated at a local mission, he changed his name to Jomo Kenyatta and moved to Nairobi where he became deeply involved in politics as an international spokesperson for African rights. From 1931 onwards, he spent 15 years in London, returning to Kenya in 1946 as the acknowledged leader of the nationalist movement. In 1953, he was arrested as a suspected Mau Mau leader and spent the next seven years in prison. On his release in 1961, he won the country's first elections as leader of KANU and at independence, in 1963, he became Prime Minister. The following year, he was made President, a position he held until his death in 1978. Known as Mzee (Father or Elder), he was not only the Father of the Kenyan nation, but one of the great heroes of African nationalism and a distinguished and respected world leader.

Statue of Mzee Jomo Kenyatta, first Prime Minister and President of independent Kenya

Culture

*K*enya has few architectural masterpieces and little visual/physical history. Until a century ago, there was no written language. Nevertheless, the country has one of the most complex and fascinating cultures in the world. People have arrived from all over Africa until today the population of about 27 million is made up of some 40 different tribes. Since the 7th century, the region has been trading with the Arabs, Persians, and Chinese, all of whom left their mark on the culture, while the arrival of the British Empire turned the whole country on its head.

In spite of this diversity, the different tribes share many characteristics and a common outlook so completely different from the European norm that bewildered settlers and visitors alike have torn their hair out in despair.

Land and wealth

The idea of money was first introduced by the British. Before that, coastal traders bartered, while the inland tribes kept their wealth in cattle and used sheep and goats as day to day currency. Hard cash has taken over now, but few Africans are willing to relinquish their herds altogether.

Among the cultivators, land is also crucial. Most tribes had strict laws of ownership and inheritance long before the Europeans came. Today, even town dwellers usually have a small garden plot or *shamba* in the country, farmed for them by their wives or families. As the population explodes, attempts to find new land to colonise are creating a whole new set of tribal confrontations.

Loyalties and leadership

Few people ever say they are Kenyan; their identity comes from their tribe, and their loyalty belongs, first and foremost, to their wives and children, and to brothers and sisters by the same mother. After that comes a duty to siblings by other mothers (many people are still polygamous), then to the extended family, and finally to clan and tribe.

Europeans go peuce about nepotism and the lack of patriotism, but the country is almost totally irrelevant and it is considered only proper that a man in authority will help his kinsfolk first.

The tribal elders and chiefs act as judge and jury, intermediary and guide. Their word is law and they are treated with enormous respect. This gives a status to old people lost in Western society, but it also undermines our view of democracy. Few dare question the decisions or actions of this supreme council, and many still vote according to the dictates of their chief.

Religion

The Masai have no religion; the coastal tribes and Somalis in the northeast are Muslim. Elsewhere, rival bands of missionaries have made Christianity a growth industry, as many people combine aspects of traditional religions with Christianity. It is easily done. Many of the traditional religions believed in one God, while they used ancestors in the same way that Catholics use saints, as conduits to God and guardians of the living. There is still a profound belief in magic and the local 'witchdoctor' will be

Fisherman in a dugout canoe, off the Mombasa coast

consulted about curses while physical ailments are handed over to Western medicine. Traditionally, in many tribes, both men and women must be circumcised, unless they are prepared to leave the tribe or remain unmarried.

The role of women

Kenyan women, from all tribes, carry the vast majority of the workload. On top of running the home and family, doing all the cooking and cleaning, fetching of water and firewood, they will do at least some of the farming and are often also responsible for physically building their house. They are respected within the home, but traditionally have no say in public affairs. If a woman returns, or is sent back to her family, her husband may remarry, but she is unlikely to and will get no further support either for herself or her children. Few women have the opportunity for any but the most basic education and only a handful have made

it on to the first rung of the career ladder. In other African countries socialism has provided sexual equality as a goal, if not a reality. In Kenya the concept is completely alien.

Samburu woman, aged by her workload

The Tribes of Kenya

*I*n Kenya, tribal, not national identity is all important. There are some 40 different tribes in the country, made up of three main groupings. The Cushites began arriving from Ethiopia and Somalia in about 2000BC and are still heading south in sporadic waves. The Nilotic tribes came down from Egypt and the Sudan from about 1000BC. The Bantu have been drifting over from West Africa since about 500BC.

The original hunter-gatherers who lived here prior to 2000BC were killed, pushed out or absorbed by intermarriage and no longer have any separate identity. The groupings are almost purely linguistic, and among the many tribes who share common roots, you can find every type of lifestyle from hunter-gatherers to nomadic herders, settled farmers and fishermen.

There are no accurate census statistics, but three tribes, the Kikuyu, the Luyia and the Luo, together make up over half of the population. Other tribes range from the Kipsigis, at 3 million, to the tiny El Molo, the smallest tribe in Kenya with about 500 members (see page 136).

The Cushites

The Cushites make up a tiny fragment of Kenya's population, clinging to survival on the fringes of habitable country in the northern deserts, the desolate Turkana area and the coastal hinterland. Among the many tribes, only the Somali number more than a few thousand. Others include the Boran, Burji, Dassenich, Gabbra, Orma, Sakuye, Boni, Wata, Yaaka, Dahalo, Galla, Rendille and El Molo.

The Nilotic tribes

There are three main sub-groups within the Nilotic tribes. One is made up of the nomadic herders – the Masai, who spread across the south of the country, the Samburu who occupy the centre, and the Turkana in the northwest (see pages 86–7). Romantic and decorative figures, there are fewer than a million all told, but they are, without doubt, the most famous people in Kenya.

Next comes a series of tiny tribes – the Kipsigis, Nandi, Tugen, Marakwet, Keiyo, Pokot, Terik and Sabaot – known collectively as the Kalenjin. Settled farmers, many of them live in the Rift Valley area, but with communities as far flung as Mt Elgon. President Moi is Tugen and through him, the Kalenjin have become a powerful political force.

Finally, in the far west, around the shores of Lake Victoria, are the farming and fishing Luo, with a population of 4.2 million, the second largest tribe in Kenya.

Giriama woman cooking *posho*

Luo fisherman mending his nets beside Lake Victoria

The Bantu

The Bantu tribes are industrious farmers who have become the largest and wealthiest of the three tribal groups. The Kikuyu alone number nearly 7 million (see pages 74–5). The majority – the Kikuyu, Embu, Meru, Mbeeri, Kamba and Tharaka – live in the Central Highlands. The Mijikenda group of nine sub-tribes (including the Giriama) lives in the coastal hinterland, while the Pokomo group of 13 sub-tribes inhabits the Tana River area. In the West are the Gusii, Suba, Kuria and the Luyia group of 17 sub-tribes.

More recent developments

The situation is still changing. The Swahili culture is a mix of the coastal Bantu peoples and Omani Arabs (see pages 106–7). There has been constant movement south from Somalia, from the violent intrusions of the Galla in the 16th century to the flood of over half a million refugees in the last few years. Intermarriage has blurred both territorial boundaries and physiological features but even so, a whole new set of tribal conflicts is brewing as overcrowded communities attempt to spill into their neighbours' lands.

Geography

*K*enya is a country put together by the British at the end of the 19th century from a whole network of tribal territories. It covers a total area of 582,750sq km, is split roughly in half by the Equator and includes every conceivable sort of terrain from snow-capped volcanoes to arid desert, with altitudes ranging from sea level to 5,199m. As well as a 480km-long coastline, about 13,600sq km of the country's area is made up of water, the great majority of this being in its share of the massive Lake Victoria (3,785sq km) and Lake Turkana (6,400sq km). Of its eight main rivers, the longest is the Tana (700km), which rises on Mount Kenya and flows across the eastern plains to the Indian Ocean.

Geology

The oldest known rocks in Kenya, dating back about 3,000 million years, are found in the plains of the south and west (Lake Victoria, the Masai Mara and Tsavo). About 1,000 million years ago, these were covered with sheets of lava which created pockets of gold-bearing granite and quartz, and the softer rhyolites, mined today as Kisii soapstone.

About 500 million years ago the land buckled, creating a vast mountain range stretching nearly 6,000km from the Middle East to Mozambique. This is the basis for Kenya's Central Highlands. Great rivers sprang from these mountain heights, wending their way across the ancient plains to the sea. As the mountains eroded, these rivers carried the sediments downstream and, from 300 million years ago onwards, laid them out across the coastal plains. From about

Desolation in the drought-stricken lava flows around Lake Turkana

180 to 70 million years ago (the heyday of the dinosaurs), this plain was invaded by the sea, which stretched far inland to where Mount Kenya now stands.

The next dramatic shift began about 70 million years ago as two parallel stretches of the largely eroded mountains began to bulge upwards, creating new ranges separated by a shallow depression. Twenty million years ago this valley began to split in a series of earthquakes and volcanic eruptions which created the Great Rift Valley (see page 58). Since then, intense volcanic activity has continued in and around the Rift, throwing up all Kenya's greatest mountains, from Mount Kenya to the crater volcanoes, such as Longonot. Most are now extinct, but there is still considerable activity under the surface. Mount Teleki, near Lake Turkana, last erupted in 1899, while the crater of Central Island, Lake Turkana, was billowing ash in the 1960s. Numerous hot springs are found along the Rift Valley and those just to the south of Lake Naivasha have recently been harnessed at the vast Olkaria geothermal power station.

Natural resources

Despite all this geological upheaval, Kenya has relatively few mineral resources. There are deposits of gold, silver, iron and lead, but the amounts are too small for profitable exploitation. Soda is mined at Lake Magadi, and there is some mining for gemstones such as garnet, but it is the fossils – coral limestone and diatomite – that have proved to be the most lucrative minerals. By far Kenya's greatest resources, however, are its fertile agricultural lands, and the wildlife and coast which bring in tourism.

A carpet of tea across the Kericho Hills in western Kenya

The economy

Kenya has a wide manufacturing base, mainly for home consumption, although some of the produce spills over into neighbouring African countries. It also acts as a trading centre for Central and East Africa, controlling much of the region's shipping and fuel distribution.

Tourism has recently become the country's greatest earner of foreign exchange, but agriculture is still the bedrock of the economy, with some 80 per cent of the population living off the land. The main cash crops are coffee and tea, sisal, pyrethrum and pineapples and, to a lesser extent, fruit and flowers, cotton, tobacco and sugar cane.

KIDS, GOATS AND GULLIES

Kenya's ecology is balanced on a knife edge. The population is rising at 3.7 per cent a year – one of the highest growth rates in the world – and the large majority of the population is under the age of 15. Polygamous families with three or four wives and 11 or 12 children are not uncommon.

Every African male expects to own his own land, or herds. The pressure on resources is already critical as marginal lands are taken into cultivation, over-grazed, and allowed to erode. Meanwhile, the north has been suffering disastrous droughts. The goats have snatched the last blade of dry grass and died, leaving their owners entirely dependent on food aid. In a terrible catch-22, it is impossible to sink boreholes to relieve the suffering because the underground water supports the last few patches of green which could regenerate the landscape when the rains eventually come.

Available water would attract the flocks, which would promptly strip the land and turn this, too, into desert. Ironically, in the fertile mountains it is water that is causing the damage, as the rain sweeps the exposed top soil into chocolate-coloured rivers.

Tourism has brought new problems, from over-development in the parks to clumsy flippers killing off the fragile coral reefs. Nevertheless, without tourism Kenya would have no national parks and most of its wildlife would have vanished. Most Africans admit openly that they would prefer to use the land for grazing. The parks are

only tolerated because the local tribes receive a percentage of the gate.

In the long term, the authorities admit that the only solution is to alter the entire traditional culture of the nation. In the short term, in Kenya at least, it seems that tourism is the saviour of a troubled land.

Left: women planting fields in Central Kenya
Top: Samburu women and children
Above, left: Masai boy herding the family cattle
Above, right: hungry goats strip the last grass from the shores of Lake Turkana

Flora

*B*right, wonderful and often weird, Kenya's flora is extraordinarily diverse, with some 10,000 species catalogued, from tiny wayside flowers to giant hardwood trees. For most casual visitors, however, the floral landscape, as it exists today, is strongly influenced by man. Away from wildlife and wilderness areas, many of the most spectacular flowering plants and trees, and nearly all the agricultural crops, have been introduced.

Garden Kenya

The Africans are rarely interested in flower gardens, preferring to use the land for more profitable purposes, but Kenya still has some wonderful gardens.

In the mid-19th century, the British ruled half the world and traded with the other half. They were also obsessive gardeners and today, one of the easiest ways of tracing their presence is by the fantastic variety of flowering plants they swapped across the globe. Urban roads were planted with trees to create superb avenues of purple jacarandah (from South America) or scarlet flame trees (from Madagascar). Garden fences are incandescent with sweeping bougainvillaea (from Brazil). From the Americas also come the bright cascades of golden shower, poinsettias, big as trees, with bracts of scarlet, pink, yellow and white, and the creamy white and yellow flowers of the frangipani. From China they imported the hibiscus bush, with its glossy leaves and huge, brilliantly coloured flowers, and from Europe they brought roses and daisies, to remind them of home.

Agricultural Kenya

The ever useful coconut floated over from Polynesia on its own, thousands of years ago, and some crops, such as sorghum and gourds, are indigenous. But the agricultural landscape of today is a largely modern, European creation, with crops ranging from maize and potatoes (originally from the Americas) to citrus (from China), tea and coffee. Even many of the working forests are now planted with quick-growing imports such as eucalyptus, brought in from Australia, and pine.

Kenya has a wide range of indigenous euphorbias, from tiny shrubs to trees

Cascades of bougainvillaea turn gardens technicolour

Indigenous plants

Kenya's indigenous species grow in a series of clearly defined altitude bands. At the lowest levels, the most interesting trees are the vast, fleshy baobabs, said to have angered the gods and been planted upside-down, and the dense, twisted mangrove that lines some areas of the coast, growing through the silt and salty water.

Between 1,000 and 1,500m, the prevailing vegetation is coarse savannah grass with some 40 different species of acacia, from small, scrubby thorn bushes to the huge yellow fever tree made famous in Rudyard Kipling's *Just So Stories*. Amid the grasses hide several species of convolvulus, aloes and a range of euphorbias from ground-hugging creepers to the cactus-like candelabra tree. These are all tough plants that have evolved protective features that enable them to survive the burning equatorial sun and the long periods of drought that ravage the land.

The forests start at about 1,500m, although little remains at this lower level. Not only is this the prime agricultural belt, but most of the great slow-growing hardwoods that thrive here, such as mahogany, teak and ebony, have been felled for timber. To find large expanses of intact forest, you have to climb above 2,500m, into the impenetrable tangle of cedar, hagenia and bamboo. This is a shadowy, green world where tiny orchids hide in knotted tree trunks, thick lianas hang like rope, flowering creepers provide sudden splashes of bright colour and grey Spanish moss drips like ancient cobwebs from the leaves.

At 3,000m, the forest ends abruptly and you come out on to open heath, where red-hot pokers, gladioli and delphiniums splash the land with colour. But these dazzling plants just form a backdrop for Africa's giant alpine species – tree heather, giant groundsel and great plumes of lobelia, 9m high. Surely these are the most wonderful plants of all.

Fauna

BIRDS

The big mammals may be the main draw to the Kenyan countryside, but in terms of variety and sheer numbers, they pale into insignificance against the country's feathered population. Kenya has no fewer than 1,033 known species of bird, more are still being discovered, and even the most humble nature trail can sometimes provide the dedicated twitcher with sightings of up to 50 different species. Kenya's birds range in size from the tiny sunbird to the huge ostrich and cover every colour of the rainbow and a few more besides.

Open savannah and woodland

Of all Kenya's birds, the 2m-tall ostrich is king, roaming the open grasslands in small family groups. The males are black with white tail feathers, the females a dusty brown. In spite of having wings, they are flightless, their body weight too great for them to lift off the ground. To compensate, they have evolved into very fast runners with a powerful kick.

Other birds to watch out for in open country include ground-living guineafowl and francolins, and tree- and ground-dwelling hornbills, with their huge, hooked bills. Tiny jewel-like sunbirds hover above the bushes; trees hang heavy with the nests of golden and crimson weaver birds. Around the lodges cluster sociable wood-hoopoes, flocks of brightly coloured waxbills, irridescent blue/black glossy starlings and brilliant superb

An ostrich family out for a stroll in Meru National Reserve

starlings with green backs, russet chests, white collars and turquoise heads.

Birds of prey and scavengers

There are seven species of vulture found in Kenya, of which the most common is the white-backed vulture with a 2.3m wingspan. Scavengers of carrion, these large, ungainly birds with hunched backs and bald heads wheel around the sky, perch on high branches or scrabble round a kill, their heads dripping in blood. The other common scavenger is the Marabou stork, nearly 2m tall, with a grey back, white front and ruff, and a bald, pink head.

There are numerous different birds of prey, including harriers, goshawks, sparrowhawks, buzzards, kites, falcons, kestrels and eagles. Look out in particular for the African fish eagle, a black, white and chestnut giant that lives near fresh water and has a haunting scream, and the huge, tawny martial eagle, with white, spotted legs, stunning for its sheer size. The leggy, crested secretary bird, which gains its name from the similarity of its features to black trousers, grey jacket and the quill pen-like feathers stuck behind its ear, stalks the grassland, preying on insects and reptiles, including small snakes.

Water birds

Of all Kenya's birdlife, the greatest concentrations are to be found along the line of the Great Rift Valley. Some of the best freshwater bird-watching is at Lake Baringo, where herons, cranes, cormorants, darters and storks perch on the rocky shoreline, eyeing their prey; several species of kingfishers, clad in black and white or turquoise, royal blue and russet, dart through the shadows; ducks, geese and moorhens bob across the ripples; and plovers, ibis and

Yellow-billed stork in the coastal mangrove swamps near Watamu

sandpipers stalk the shallows.

The alkaline soda lakes, such as Turkana or Nakuru, provide a whole new set of birds. One of the greatest sights the country has to offer is the massive sheets of thousands of pink flamingos carpeting the shallow lakes, while clouds of pelicans skim the surface of the water.

This round-up only covers the tinest fragment of Kenya's teeming birdlife. Those interested in learning more should buy the Collins *Field Guide to the Birds of East Africa*. If you plan to do any serious bird-watching, you will also need a good pair of binoculars. Many of the lodges and hotels in the best bird-watching areas will provide lists of species seen locally, guided walks with ornithologists, and some tour companies (see page 189) will even run bird-watching safaris.

MAMMALS

Kenya boasts some 160 species of mammals. It is obviously impossible to describe them all here, so this list concentrates on the more common and visible species. Those who wish to know more should read the Collins *Field Guide to the Larger Mammals of Africa*.

ANTELOPE

Bushbuck *Tragelaphus scriptus*
A smallish animal (80cm at the shoulder), the bushbuck's rump is higher

The gentle and gregarious impala, in Tsavo West National Park

than the shoulders giving it a hunched appearance. It has white patches on the neck and white spots on the flanks. Males have slightly twisted, 30cm-long horns. There are 40 different sub-species, ranging in colour from light chestnut with white stripes to a dull greyish brown. Nocturnal, they live alone in well-watered woodland across the country.

Dik-dik *Rhynchotragus kirki/guentheri*
There are two species in Kenya, both minute and dainty (30–40cm high and weighing 3–5kg), with a greyish brown coat and tiny, straight horns (males only). Guenther's are slightly smaller than Kirk's. They live alone or in pairs in savannah and scrub.

Eland *Taurotragus oryx*
Huge (2m at the shoulder) with a tawny, cow-like body, a dewlap at the neck, faint white stripes across the back, and black hair along the spine and under the belly. Males and females have long, backward-lying horns with a tight spiral at the base. They live in large herds in open savannah, mainly in the Samburu region.

Gerenuk *Litocranius walleri*
A smallish gazelle (80cm at the shoulder) with a russet back, tawny sides and white underbelly. There are white rings and black tear-drops around the eyes. Known as 'giraffe-necked' because of its elongated neck. Males have curved, ringed horns. They live alone or in small groups in the dry northern scrub and stand on their hind legs to feed.

Grant's gazelle *Gazella granti*
A medium-sized gazelle (up to 90cm at the shoulders), with a tawny back,

slightly darker stripe along the flanks, and white underbelly. There is a white patch, outlined in black around the tail. The face has whitish stripes from eye to nose. Males and females have long, ridged, bent horns. They live in small herds in dry scrubland in Tsavo and the north.

Hartebeest *Alcelaphus buselaphus*
A large, distinctive animal (160cm at the shoulder), with a uniform tan coat and steeply sloping back. It has a very long narrow face, a stupid expression and thick, ridged horns shaped like a candelabrum. They live in large herds in open grassland and are widely distributed across Kenya.

Impala *Aepyceros melampus*
The largest of Kenya's gazelles (1m at the shoulder). They have a russet back, paler sides and a white underbelly. There are black stripes on the tail and rump, and the face is tawny with a darker strip along the nose. The males have long, lyre-shaped horns. They live in large

Grant's gazelle, a desert lover able to survive for months without water

herds in open grassland and are found in most areas of the country. Renowned athletes, they can jump heights of up to 3m and have recorded speeds of 96km/h.

The huge, elegant sable antelope is rare in Kenya, found only at Shimba Hills

OTHER ANTELOPE TO LOOK OUT FOR:
Bongo: chestnut with white stripes and long horns, and up to 120cm high. Rare, timid, and nocturnal, living in high montane forest.
Duiker: fawny grey, up to 60cm tall. There are four species in Kenya. Common, but rarely seen as they are nocturnal and live in dense woodland and long grass.
Roan antelope: the size of a horse, uniformly tan, with a black and white face and swept-back ridged horns. Rare in Kenya, found in the Lambwe Valley and Shimba Hills.

Sable antelope: a glossy black giant with huge sickle-shaped horns, white underparts and stripy face. Found only in the Shimba Hills.
Sitatunga: like a shaggy, darker bushbuck in appearance. Very rare; found only at Lake Victoria and Saiwa Swamp.

The rare, striped lesser kudu is found mainly in southeast Kenya

Klipspringer *Oreotragus oreotragus*
Small (50cm at the shoulder) with a long, bristly coat of speckled yellowish grey and whitish underbelly. The triangular face has black and white rings around the eyes and large, black-rimmed ears. Males have short, ridged horns. They walk on tiptoe, are agile climbers and live in rocky mountains in small groups.

Lesser kudu *Tragelaphus imberbis*
Large (110cm at the shoulder), with a brownish grey coat and up to 15 narrow white stripes across the back. The head is darker with a white chevron between the eyes and two white patches on the neck. Males have long, loosely spiralling horns. They live in dense acacia scrubland in pairs or small groups, mainly in the southeast. The **greater kudu** (*Tragelaphus strepsiceros*), found only at Lake Bogoria and Marsabit, is larger (150cm at the shoulder) with 8–10 white stripes and a beard.

Oribi *Ourebia ourebi*
Small (60cm at the shoulder), with a light chestnut coat, white underbelly, large black-tipped ears and white rings around the eyes. Males have short, spiky horns. They live in small groups in long grass throughout Kenya.

Oryx *Oryx beisa*
Large (120cm at the shoulder), reddish tan with a white underbelly, black stripes along the spine and flanks, and black garters round the front legs. The face is black and white, and both males and females have very long, straight ridged horns. They live in large herds in open scrub in northern Kenya.

Bohor reedbuck *Redunca redunca*
Small (90cm at the shoulder) with a thick, bright tan coat, white underbelly and chin, and paler circles around the eyes. Males have short, stubby, forward-curving horns. They live in pairs in long

PRIMATES
Vervet monkeys (*Cercopithecus aethiops*) are the smallest of Kenya's four main species of primates. They have brown backs, lighter stomachs and dark faces, and little fear of people, often hanging around hotels. **Olive baboons** (*Papio anubis*) are

also common, living in large troops in open woodland. They are much bigger, with a yellowy brown coat and square dog-like face. They can be dangerous. Much rarer are the monkey species that dwell in the high montane forests. The **blue monkey** (*Cercopithecus mitis*) is thick-set with a dense bluish grey coat, black legs and black band around the shoulders, and long white whiskers around the face. Most beautiful of all is the **Abyssinian black-and-white colobus monkey** (*Colobus abyssinicus*) which is large, jet black, with a white muzzle, white fringed cape across the back and long white plume at the end of the tail.

Top: baboon mother and baby
Right: oryx herd in northern scrubland

grass near water throughout Kenya. The less common **mountain reedbuck** (*Redunca fulvorufula*) has a greyish, woolly coat. It lives in small herds in rocky mountains and scrub.

Defassa waterbuck *Kobus defassa*
Large (130cm at the shoulder), with a shaggy, dark greyish brown coat, a white muzzle and white patch under the chin, the waterbuck's most distinguishing feature is a large white patch on the rump. The males have long, thickly ridged, curving horns. The **common waterbuck** (*Kobus ellipsiprymnus*) has a white circle on its rump. Both live in small herds in open woodland and marsh.

Thomson's gazelle *Gazella thomsoni*
Small (60cm at the shoulder) with a light chestnut coat, white underparts, and black stripes along the flanks and on the

rump. The face is whitish with a darker streak down the nose and black stripes along the cheeks. Males and females have fairly long, ridged and slightly curved horns. They live in large herds in open grassland throughout Kenya.

Topi *Damaliscus korrigum*
Large (130cm at the shoulder) with a sleek, dark-chestnut coat, long face, and large purplish smudges on the nose, legs and rump. They live in large herds in open grassland, but in Kenya are only found in the Masai Mara.

THE GOLDEN HORN

Since the Greek astronomer Ptolemy first visited the coast in the 2nd century AD, East Africa has been trading in ivory and rhino horn, which was thought by the Chinese to be an aphrodisiac and by the Arabs, a symbol of manhood. For centuries the situation remained stable. But with the arrival of the Europeans all that was to change.

Armed with high-powered hunting rifles, thousands set off on safari, shooting anything that moved. By the 1930s, they were game spotting from the air while the desperate elephants moved into the forests, or tried to hide the large tuskers in a herd of younger animals.

In 1977, with elephant and rhino numbers at an alarmingly low level, Kenya finally banned their hunting, but the new scarcity of rhino horn and ivory led to soaring prices. At its peak, ivory was worth about US$300 and rhino horn over US$2,000 a kilo. With such glittering prizes at stake, the poachers began a wholesale slaughter, using machine guns and helicopters, and paying officials to turn a blind eye. A decade

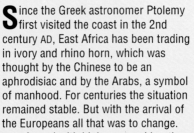

Above: an increasingly rare live black rhino.
Left: ivory hunter in *La Chasse Illustrées* (1875).

of confiscated tusks, and began to reorganise, giving its rangers military training and equipment and instituting a shoot to kill policy. It has been remarkably successful. Prices have plummeted, Kenya's rhinos all have their own personal guards, and elephant stocks are rising. The triumphant authorities are determined to keep the ban in place, in fear of renewed poaching. Desperate to avoid culling, they have experimented with contraceptive pills for elephants. Today, they are concentrating on translocating animals to parks with spare capacity – a difficult and expensive solution.

Left: Kenya celebrates the 1989 ivory ban by burning its stockpile. Below: child's conservation poster at the Langata Giraffe Sanctuary

on, Kenya had lost nearly two-thirds of its elephants, some 1,500 a year were being shot, and rhino stocks were down to a couple of hundred.

In 1989, a worldwide ban on ivory and horn was enforced. Kenya made a massive, dramatic bonfire

The reticulated giraffe is recognisable by its darker, more even patching

Giraffe *Giraffa camelopardalis*

Living in herds of up to 70 in open woodland, giraffes are graceful creatures measuring up to 6m tall, that move with a peculiar rocking-horse gallop. The most common race is the southern **Masai giraffe**, with a light tan coat and smudgy, irregular brown spots. The rare, western race, **Rothschild giraffe** has white socks and a more pronounced bump on the forehead, while the males have four horns. The **reticulated giraffe** is a separate species found in Samburu, and has a paler undercoat and crisply defined, dark-red crazy paving.

Hippopotamus *Hippopotamus amphibius*

Up to 1.7m high at the shoulder, hippos have enormous barrel bodies completely out of proportion to their short legs. They spend their days in the water, in sociable huddles, coming out to graze at night. Generally placid, they can be dangerous if disturbed. If you see one yawn – a cavernous experience – you can believe the stories of them biting a canoe in half.

Rhinoceros

Now extremely rare, rhinos live alone or in pairs in a variety of habitats from open scrub to dense montane forest. There are two species, the **black rhino** (*Diceros bicornis*), indigenous to Kenya, and the **white rhino** (*Ceratotherium simum*), which is imported for restocking from southern Africa. Both are the same colour, but the black is smaller, with a pointed upper lip. White comes from the Afrikaans word *weiss*, meaning wide, and the true name of the species is the square-lipped rhino.

PLAINS ANIMALS

Buffalo *Syncerus caffer*

Huge, ox-like creatures, up to 2m tall at the shoulder, with a dark-brown coat and short, heavy horns like a viking helmet. They live in a variety of habitats from thick forest, where they stay in small groups, to open grassland where they gather in large herds. Seemingly placid, they can be very bad-tempered if aroused.

Elephant *Loxodonta africana*

The African elephant is the world's largest land mammal, reaching heights of 3.3m at the shoulder, with tusks up to 3m long. They live up to 70 years, are highly intelligent and have sophisticated social behaviour. Herds vary from family groups of five or six to over 100, and they adapt to many habitats from open plains to thick forest. The elephant's nearest relative is the tiny, rabbit-like **rock hyrax**.

Herd of Burchell's (common) zebras, usually seen in the company of antelope and wildebeest

Warthog *Phacochoerus aethiopicus*
A small and intensely ugly bush pig, the warthog has a greyish skin, with a dark mane, an elongated snout with lumpy warts above the eyes and on the cheeks, and small, upward curving tusks. They live in open grassland, in nuclear families, and stick their tails up like flags when they run.

Wildebeest *Connochaetes taurinus*
Technically an antelope, the wildebeest, or brindled gnu, has been described as having 'the forequarters of an ox, the hindquarters of an antelope and the tail of a horse'. Measuring up to 1.5m at the shoulder, they have a greyish brown coat, huge, dark head with a straggly mane and beard, and small, thick horns that meet across the forehead. They are very gregarious, gathering in vast herds for the migration (see also page 85).

Zebra
There are two species of these black and white striped wild horses in Kenya. The more common is **Burchell's zebra** (*Equus* [*Hippogritis*] *burchelli*), with broad, uneven striping. **Grevy's zebra** (*Equus* [*Dolichohippus*] *grevyi*) is found only in the Samburu region. It has many thin, symmetrical pop-art stripes, a white belly and large, rounded ears. Both are gregarious, mixing in large herds in open grassland.

THE BIG FIVE
For a really successful game-viewing trip, it is said that you should see 'The Big Five' – lion, elephant, rhino, buffalo and leopard. All are present in Kenya's main parks, but rhinos are very rare and leopards very shy.

PREDATORS

Cheetah *Acinonyx jubatus*
Tawny, with round, black spots, and a small, neat head with black stripes round the muzzle, the cheetah is sleek and elegant, built for speed. They have clocked record-breaking speeds of up to 112kph over 400m. They live in small groups in open savannah and hunt usually in the early morning.

Jackal
Small, fox-like animals that survive by scavenging and hunting small animals. Largely nocturnal, they live in small packs in open savannah. There are three species in Kenya, all with brown to yellowish grey coats: the **golden jackal** (*Canis aureus*); the **side-striped** (*Canis adustus*) with a white stripe along the flanks; and the **black-backed** (*Canis mesomelas*) with a black back!

Leopard *Panthera pardus*
Long, low and immensely powerful, the leopard has clustered rings of dark spots on a rich red-gold background. Living solitary lives in rocky hills and woodland, they are nocturnal hunters and spend the days hiding in caves or high branches.

Lion *Panthera leo*
The largest of the great cats of Africa, lions can reach up to 90cm in height at the shoulder, and have a uniform tawny coloured coat. Only the males have manes. They usually live in prides of 10 to 20 animals, in open savannah. Males make a lot of noise, but the females do all the work, hunting at night or dawn. They all spend the day resting from the heat.

Spotted hyena *Crocuta crocuta*
A large, dog-like animal with a powerful head and shoulders, a steeply sloping back and weak backlegs, the hyena has a scruffy, tawny coat with blackish spots. Efficient scavengers, they also prey on small or feeble animals. They generally live in small packs, but gather in large groups before mating and sometimes set up nurseries for the young. Largely nocturnal, they have a range of distinctive cries, from piercing howls to a terrifyingly eerie laugh.

Male lion at a kill in the Masai Mara

FIRST STEPS

'*Kenya grapples with its identity with a blend of pain and panache that only Africa can manage.*'

MORT ROSENBLUM AND DOUG WILLIAMSON,
Squandering Eden (1987)

PLANNING YOUR ITINERARY

Kenya is one of those extraordinary crossroads countries that really does provide something for everyone and it can be difficult to work out an itinerary, or select a package, because there is just too much choice. This is a basic, subjective list of where to find the very best the country has to offer.

Beaches: Watamu, just south of Malindi, with silver white sand, rich coral reefs, and little seaweed.
Bird watching: the Rift Valley, particularly Lake Baringo for over 300 species including flamingos and pelicans; the Kakamega Forest in western Kenya for rare, rainforest species; the Malindi area for coastal birds.
Fishing: the Aberdares for mountain rivers; Lake Victoria; and the Malindi/Watamu region for deep-sea fishing.
Food: Nairobi, Mombasa, Nyali (just north of Mombasa), and Lamu.
Game-viewing: the Masai Mara, particularly during the wildebeest migration (between July and October); Amboseli, for a concentration of game in a small area.
Hiking: Mount Kenya, the Aberdares and Mount Elgon for heavy-duty mountain walking; the Ewaso Nyiro river area near Maralal for easier trekking and camel-supported walking safaris.
History: Lamu, Gedi and Mombasa old town for Arabic history; Nairobi and the Rift Valley for prehistoric and colonial history.
Nightlife: Nairobi, Nyali.
Rugged adventure: Lake Turkana.
Scenery: the Aberdares and Mount Elgon for mountain scenery and vegetation; the Limuru area for views over the Rift Valley escarpment and volcanoes; the area around Kisii in western Kenya for intensively farmed terraces; Amboseli for the views of Mount Kilimanjaro; Lake Turkana for bleak, dramatic desertscapes; the Kilifi area for coastal creeks.

Fishing canoes pulled up on to the sandy beach near Malindi

Flocks of flamingos wading in the shallow waters of a Rift Valley soda lake

Tribal peoples: the Masai in the area surrounding the Masai Mara; Maralal area for the Samburu; Lake Turkana for the Turkana and El Molo people.

LIVING WITH KENYA

Etiquette

On the whole, Kenyans are extremely polite, friendly and hospitable people. Always ask after the person's health and introduce yourself at the start of any proper conversation. Call a man *Bwana* (Mister) or a woman *Mama* (Mother or Madam), as a term of respect.

In the higher levels of society – and in white homes – Western rules of hospitality apply; if you are invited for a meal, take a small gift. But if you are invited into a village home, be prepared to eat and live as the family does and don't reject their food once you have accepted the invitation. Offer to pay for your board and, above all, remember that these are poor people. Don't abuse their welcome by living at their expense for days on end.

Africans touch more than Westerners do. They always shake hands on meeting, and men will often hold hands in the street. This is not a sign of homosexuality, but of trust.

You may be asked some staggeringly personal questions, but this is usually only curiosity, so deflect them with a smile and don't get upset. Race is the one truly touchy area and most Africans prefer to avoid the subject altogether. Their memory stretches back to colonial days and they can be quick to find offence even where none is intended.

The lifestyle is casual, but do not wander around the towns in beach wear. The up-market city hotels may ask men to wear a jacket and tie after sundown. The coastal region is almost solidly Muslim and nude or topless sunbathing is a grave insult as well as being illegal.

Visitors under siege from enthusiastic souvenir sellers

The hassle factor

One of the most tiring aspects of the country is the general belief that all Westerners are super-rich. There is relatively little open begging, but you will be constantly surrounded by people hoping to sell you their wares or asking for help to pay their school fees, provide pens, books, or sweets for the children. Your heart will often bleed at the very real need surrounding you, but for the sake of your own sanity and solvency, you must have iron-clad resolution and only buy or give when you really want to.

If you do show any interest in buying, the price will be set according to what they think you might be prepared to pay and you will find yourself involved in protracted haggling, often with half a dozen people. Once you do eventually buy from one, the next will step forward to try and persuade you to buy from them as well. They do not understand that if you have already bought 10 bracelets, you do not need any more, and will point out patiently that you have not yet bought a bracelet from them. There are no easy answers.

Language

Kenya has 40 tribes, all with their own languages. The official language of the country is Swahili, which is spoken by almost everyone except a few of the nomads. English is almost as widely spoken, however, and unless you are way off the beaten track, you will always find someone who speaks enough to help you. On the coast you will also find that resort receptionists and the souvenir sellers often have a smattering of German, French and Italian. Surviving is easy, but it is considered good manners to learn at least a few words of Swahili as a token gesture.

Servants

Kenyan society still survives, to some extent, in a colonial mode and unless you are roughing it in the cheapest possible way, get used to being surrounded by fleets of servants. Even mid-range camping trips regard as essential a driver, a cook and sometimes a couple of other people to collect firewood, put up tents and heat water. Most of them speak very good English, and are a mine of useful and interesting information.

It is easy to get used to wallowing in luxury, but do remember that the staff work long, very hard days. They will stay on duty until you go to bed, and they will rarely refuse to do anything you ask of them, even if they know that it is not sensible. They have to obey your wishes or risk losing their jobs. It is up to you to think of their comfort as well as your own.

Women travellers

Travelling alone as a woman is as safe as for any man, as long as you obey the most basic rules of security. It can also be extremely rewarding. In a country that has barely heard the word liberation, women travellers, with a lifestyle that can seem to come from another planet, have a particular curiosity value. If you are careful, you can get the best of both worlds, being treated by the African men as an 'honorary man', and having access to the women that men are denied.

Western women suffer relatively little from harassment and any that does occur is usually good humoured and rarely persistent. There is some danger of rape in the cities, so don't walk around after dark. Women should also keep a little distance from the men unless they are genuinely interested, as few Africans have any concept of platonic friendship between men and women, and it is very easy to dig yourself into a complicated situation.

Above: click! click! but use consideration and tact when taking photographs of people, and offer to pay. Below: many traditional crafts, such as this Masai beadwork, are fast degenerating into tourist tat

Mombasa Station, beginning of the Lunatic Line, Kenya's charming but under-used railway

GETTING AROUND

Look at a map of Kenya and the country seems remarkably accessible, with highways, main roads and plentiful minor roads, a good rail network and numerous airfields. Nor are distances too long. All things are relative, however, and something marked as a highway in Kenya is probably the equivalent of a minor B road in Europe. It might even be marked as the main road simply because it is the only road. A 200km journey might take three hours, but it might also take three days.

By air

By far the easiest and fastest way to get around is by air, often in small planes that offer spectacular views. There are reasonably priced scheduled flights to most towns and game parks, and even hiring a charter flight is not excessively priced if several of you share the cost.

By rail

While the railway looks impressive, there is only one train a day each way between Nairobi and Mombasa and between Nairobi and Kisumu. A rail journey is, however, an experience in itself (see page 146).

By road

The road system is terrible. Even the tarred roads are bumpy while the dirt roads often descend into cavernous pot-holes linked by corrugations.

Because of the wear and tear, car hire is very expensive. Consider hiring a driver along with your car. It is safer if you have a knowledgeable local around; it is not much more expensive and you also get an excellent unofficial tour guide and game spotter, and someone to cope with the inevitable punctures and breakdowns. Take advise about security before setting out. Public transport on the roads consists of a few battered buses and a huge number of lethal and horribly overcrowded *matatus* (shared taxis). The cheapest way to get around safely and see the best of the country is to join an organised safari.

For more information on getting around, see **Practical Guide**, pages 180–1 and 189.

SURVIVING KENYA

Health

In the pecking order of developing countries, Kenya is one of the safest and most hygienic, and as long as you are sensible you stand little chance of being ill. Nevertheless, this is a tropical country that is host to a wide range of diseases, many unpleasant and some fatal, and as a Westerner, you will have little or no natural immunity.

A full set of inoculations is essential and should include protection against yellow fever, typhoid, tetanus, hepatitis and polio. Start the course two months prior to your visit. Secondly, and crucially, take anti-malarial prophylaxes. Malaria is endemic and deadly. As the pills are not 100 per cent reliable, also arm yourself with a supply of repellent, mosquito coils, and a mosquito net, and cover yourself up in the evenings. The best way to avoid getting malaria is not to get bitten.

The water in the main towns and resort hotels is usually safe to drink. Once out of town, or lower down the social scale, don't ever drink tap water, unless you purify it yourself. At tourist establishments, food is usually scrupulously hygienic but, again, once outside the cocoon be sensible about what you eat. Don't swim in any natural fresh water because you risk picking up bilharzia, and don't walk around barefoot,

Brightly coloured and often lethal *matatus* are Kenya's main form of public transport

as there are numerous small, nasty worms and insects on the ground. Abstain from casual sex or take a good supply of heavy-duty condoms. Aids is rife.

If you get any open wounds, treat them with antiseptic and cover them up. If bitten by any animal, get treatment for rabies immediately. Take a pack of sterile needles and use them if you need an injection. If you need a transfusion, get to the best possible hospital, or preferably, return home first. If you are ill after you get home, remember to tell your doctor you have been in the tropics.

Kenya's roads leave a lot to be desired – this would count as a major thoroughfare

Safety and security

Sadly, Kenya suffers from a high crime rate and tourists are sometimes targeted as the richest pickings. Don't let this deter you from going, however; if you are sensible, you should be fine.

In town, you are most at risk from muggers and pick-pockets. Wearing a money belt will not necessarily help as the more determined muggers simply slash through the strap. Whenever possible, leave valuables in the hotel safe, don't take more money than you need and if stopped, hand it over. It is better to end up poorer than in hospital. Use a handbag with a zip and shoulder strap for slinging diagonally, and carry your wallet in an inside or front pocket. Check with locals about which areas are safe and, most importantly, never walk anywhere after dark. Take a taxi even if you are only going a couple of blocks.

In the rural areas, Kenya's chief problem is bandits, most of whom are armed refugees from its neighbouring states – Sudan, Ethiopia, Uganda, Somalia and Tanzania, all of which have, or have had, severe problems of famine, drought or civil war. Security within the national parks has been stepped right up and these are now safe. There are problems on some roads, however, and tourist buses are occasionally held up at gun point. Just

bear in mind that the country is desperate to ensure that tourists are safe and is doing everything in its power to mop up the bandits. A convoy system operates on some of the more dangerous roads while tourists are advised to avoid some areas altogether. Listen carefully to what the locals say and take their advice. If you are travelling independently, hire a car with a driver and always make sure you reach your destination by dusk.

Surviving in the wild

It may seem like a stupid truism, but the first rule is to remember *wild animals are wild*. They are therefore dangerous and if they feel threatened or provoked in any way, will not hesitate to attack. If you did escape with no more than a bite, there is a chance that the animal is diseased. In the national parks and on safari, you will be shepherded around by guides and game guards and will often feel frustrated by seemingly pointless rules. Just remember that the rules are there for a purpose – to protect your life.

There are a few absolutely basic rules to survival:

1 Do not get out of the car near animals, no matter how dopey they seem. The placid looking hippo grazing on the mudflats could literally chomp you

Many Nairobi inhabitants now hire private security guards (askaris)

SNAKES

Visit any one of Kenya's proliferation of snake parks and you will see and even handle all you desire, but although there are plenty in the wild, most are shy and you will rarely see them. Many prefer a hot, dry habitat with plenty of rocks and sand, as at Lake Turkana and Tsavo, but there are also forest species, such as the deadly **Gaboon viper** and the tree-dwelling **boomslang** in lowland forests such as Kakamega and Arabuko-Sokoke. Of the poisonous snakes, look out in particular for the following three species: **spitting cobras**; short, sluggish **puff adders** which rely on camouflage, do not move out of your way, and are easy to tread on; and **black mambas** (actually dark grey to olive brown, with a black inner mouth) which are shy, but actively bad-tempered and may well strike first.

Pythons are the largest and most dramatic of all the snakes, reaching lengths of up to 6m. Although they look alarming, they are not poisonous, only eat every few months, and are harmless to humans.

The puff adder relies on its remarkable camouflage and is easily trodden on

in half if she feels her calf is under threat.

2 Never feed any wild animal, no matter how cute or persistent. That sweet little monkey has razor-sharp teeth that can bite to the bone.

3 If you are out of your vehicle and your guide tells you to move, move first and ask questions later. His eyes are far better at spotting well-camouflaged animals than yours and he could have seen a lion in that nearby clump of grass.

4 If you go out walking, always wear trousers and sensible shoes, watch where you put your feet and hands, and check the ground or the rock before you sit down. You could find yourself confronted by a snake, scorpion or poisonous spider.

5 If you do get bitten by anything, get *immediate* medical help. Some snakes can kill within 30 minutes. Treatment for an animal bite should include a tetanus booster and rabies shots.

6 If camping, shake out your sleeping bag before you get in, and tap out your shoes in the morning. Spiders and scorpions find these objects welcome retreats!

This section may sound alarmist. Please remember while reading it that Kenya is a fabulous country and that your journey will be one of the greatest experiences of your life. Don't let the need for a little common sense put you off going. For more detailed practical information, see **Practical Guide**, pages 176–89.

Many people are happy to be photographed, as long as you pay first

PHOTOGRAPHY

Kenya is an amazingly photogenic country. The scenery is superb, the people are beautiful, and, much of the time, the light is wonderful. Best of all, the parks abound with animals so used to cameras that they almost line up to pose, best profile to the fore. Work out how much film you think you are going to need, double the amount, then double it again. 200 ISO film is probably the best for general purposes, but take some faster film as well for shots of moving animals, heavy midday shadows and the fabulous sunsets. Remember that the best game-viewing hours are early morning and late afternoon. To have any hope of taking good wildlife shots, you will need at least a 300mm lens.

Film of all types is readily available in Nairobi, Mombasa and most resort hotels. It is also possible to get photos developed in Nairobi and Mombasa, including 1-hour and 1-day fast services.

Sadly, but inevitably, the Kenyan people have learned their photographic value all too well and almost nobody will let you take a picture of them without cash up front – usually 10 or 20 shillings per person. This can even apply if you are shooting general street scenes or you happen to include people by accident in the background of a shot. The Masai and Samburu are particularly hot on this and people who have tried to take a couple of surreptitious pictures have ended up at the wrong end of a spear. If you want to photograph the people, ask them first as a matter of courtesy and be prepared to negotiate a price.

Taking photos of anything to do with the police, military or the state is strictly illegal and you could lose your film, your camera, or even end up in jail.

A fish eagle, talons extended, swoops down on an unsuspecting fish

WHAT TO SEE

'Africa is mystic; it is wild; it is
a sweltering inferno; it is a
photographer's paradise, a
hunter's Valhalla, an escapist's
Utopia. It is what you will,
and it withstands all
interpretations.'

BERYL MARKHAM,
West with the Night (1942)

NAIROBI CITY CENTRE

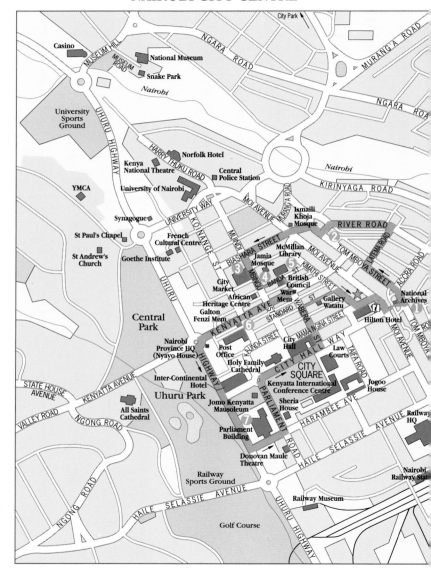

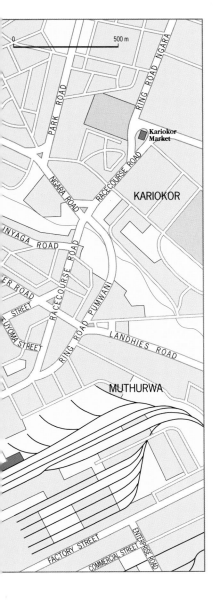

Nairobi

*I*n May 1899, construction of the East African Railway (see pages 144–5) reached a high plateau, known to the Masai as Nyrobi (the place of cool waters). It had glutinous black soil and was swampy and fever-ridden, but it was the last flat land before the Rift Valley and a suitable site for a railhead. By July, the population was nearing 20,000.

In 1900, Nairobi officially became a town. In 1907, the town became capital of British East Africa. By the 1950s, it had acquired a glamorous Bohemian image that fed on the great Hollywood stars and titled aristocracy who flocked here on safari.

Today, Nairobi has a population of 2.5 million. In the tiny tree-lined city centre, peeling colonial buildings huddle under sharply pristine skyscrapers. The first impression is of chaos and decay; after a week in the bush, it seems a hive of sophistication and elegance. Around this heart sprawl up-market suburbs, with elegant houses and gardens festooned with bougainvillaea. Between the city centre and the suburbs vast soulless tenements have been built in an effort to clear the slums. Around these, miles of new slums spring up daily.

Nairobi is all things to all people – the capital of a nation; the finest city in black Africa; the start of a dream; and the epitome of despair. You can buy anything here from Gucci watches to *foie gras*. Those that don't have money are mainly concerned with extracting it from those that do. Most visitors see it as a convenient stop between the airport and game parks.

Nairobi's skyline is changing from one of low colonial buildings to a nest of skyscrapers

CITY PARK

Created in 1904 as Nairobi's first public park, this is a lush, cool 120-hectare area of mature forest reserve and wonderful gardens. It is home to the **Boscawen Memorial Orchid Collection** and a war cemetery containing the graves of 97 East African soldiers, mainly from World War II. More cheerfully, it also has a children's playground in a sunken garden, a maze and a bandstand. Be careful in daylight and don't go in after dark.
City Park Road, off Limuru Road, 3.5km northeast of the city centre. Open: Monday, 10am–6pm; Friday, 7am–2pm; all other days, noon–6pm. Admission charge (small).

GALLERY WATATU

A commercial gallery, this is one of a handful of places to see good quality art, with revolving displays by some 30 artists from across Africa as well as regular solo exhibitions of paintings and sculpture.
Standard Street, PO Box 41855 (tel: 225 666). Open: Monday to Saturday, 9am–6pm; Sunday, 10am–5pm. Admission free.

KENYATTA INTERNATIONAL CONFERENCE CENTRE

Built in 1974, this 28-storey (105m) building is Kenya's only major conference venue. It has an auditorium for 4,000 and is also the headquarters of KANU, the ruling political party. There are spectacular views across the city from the roof-top walkway.
City Square, PO Box 30746 (tel: 332 383 or fax: 220 349). Regular escorted tours run from Monday to Friday, between 9.30am and 12.30pm, and 2pm and 4.30pm. Admission free.

NATIONAL ARCHIVES

The archives are housed in neo-classical splendour in one of Nairobi's oldest buildings (built in 1906 for the Bank of India). The entrance hall contains a fascinating jumble of art heaped like an Aladdin's cave. The private collection of former Vice-President Joseph Murumbi, it ranges from Persian carpets and Indian chests to African masks and drums from across the continent, together with a number of paintings. Upstairs, an uninspired exhibition of archive material has some interesting information on Kenyan heroes and national emblems, but concentrates rather too heavily on politicians.

Moi Avenue, PO Box 49210 (tel: 228 959). Opposite the Hilton Hotel. Open: Monday to Friday, 8am–5pm; Saturday, 8am–2pm. Admission free.

NATIONAL MUSEUM OF KENYA

An excellent, wide-ranging museum that is the one essential sightseeing stop in central Nairobi. It has the normal selection of geological displays and dead birds and animals. The most famous of these is the life-size model of Kenyatta's favourite elephant, Ahmed, from Marsabit. Placed under 24-hour guard by presidential decree, the elephant became a national symbol of the fight against poaching. He died of natural causes in 1974, at the age of between 55 and 62, with massive tusks a full 3m long and weighing 67 kilos each.

The highlight of the museum is the Prehistory Hall. Here are the skulls which have shaped the world-wide theory of prehistory, pushing back the origins of man over 2.5 million years. Also on display is the most complete early skeleton ever found, a *Homo erectus* boy, dating back about 1.6 million years. Along with the clear explanations of East African prehistory, with their mind-boggling dates, there are copies of some of Tanzania's finest rock paintings, made by Mary and Louis Leakey in 1951; a section on Richard Leakey's Koobi Fora excavations of the 1970s (see page 136); and a series of tableaux suggesting how our earliest ancestors looked and lived.

Other interesting halls include displays on the lifestyles and traditions

of all Kenya's major tribes, a set of beautiful flower paintings by Joy Adamson (of *Born Free* fame, see pages 63 and 130), a small museum devoted to the Mau Mau and a gallery of modern Kenyan fine art.

Museum Road, off Museum Hill (tel: 742 131/4). Approx 2km northwest of the city centre, off Uhuru Highway. Open: daily, 9.30am–6pm. Guided bird tours: every Wednesday at 8.45am. Admission charge.

The 28-storey Kenyatta International Conference Centre, Nairobi

Jacarandas in bloom on Kenyatta Avenue, central Nairobi

PARLIAMENT BUILDING

This rather disappointing 1930s building is the home of Kenya's single Parliamentary House. The interior is more imposing, however. Among its artistic treasures are the 1968 statue of Kenyatta in the forecourt; the wooden panel on the landing, made by the local Kabete School in the 1950s, with each of its 32 pieces in a different local hardwood; and the series of 49 tapestries in the Long Gallery. Presented by the East African Women's League in 1968, the tapestries tell the colonial history of Kenya. Jomo Kenyatta (see page 11) is buried in a mausoleum in the gardens,

constantly attended by a guard of honour. *Parliament Road (tel: 221 291). Phone the Sergeant-at-Arms for an appointment to tour the building or for a seat in the public gallery. Admission free.*

PAYAPAA ARTS CENTRE

Founded by one of Kenya's leading artists, the effervescent and enthusiastic Elimo Njau, this is a working artists' studio used by painters and sculptors. It also has a permanent collection and sales gallery. The aim of the centre is to promote a real creativity that will lift Kenyan art out of its current rut. A motto above the main door reads 'Copying puts God to sleep'.
Ridgeways Road, off Kiambu Road, PO Box 49646 (tel: 512 257). About 8km northeast of the city centre. Open: Monday to Friday, 9am–5pm; Saturday, 2pm–5pm. Admission charge.

RAILWAY MUSEUM

This fascinating museum is dedicated to the history of the Lunatic Line (see pages 144–5). Numerous photographs and other memorabilia are used to construct the railway's past, such as the seat which was attached to the locomotive's cow-catcher to give distinguished visitors, including Winston Churchill and Theodore Roosevelt, the very best possible view. Outside are countless old engines and carriages, many in sad need of restoration. Look for number 12, the carriage in which the ill-fated Charles Ryall sat up one night, waiting for the man-eating lion which was terrorizing the work gangs during the building of the line. The unfortunate man fell asleep, was dragged from the coach and became the lion's next meal.
Ngaira Avenue (tel: 21211). Open: daily, 8.30am–4.30pm. Admission charge.

SNAKE PARK

A small park with a varied selection of East African snakes, from pythons to mambas; tortoises and crocodiles; and a small aquarium to introduce you to the freshwater tilapia which you will see more frequently on your dinner plate. *Beside the National Museum on Museum Hill, 2km northwest of the city centre, off Uhuru Highway. (tel: 742 131/4). Open: daily, 9.30am–6.30pm. Admission charge.*

UHURU PARK AND CENTRAL PARK

A dead loss in horticultural terms, this large green area is one of Nairobi's favourite weekend hang-outs. The focal point of Uhuru Park is a small boating lake, while Centre Park is dominated by the **Nyayo Monument**, built in 1988 to mark the first decade of President Moi's rule. Its vast octagonal plinth is topped by the peaks of Mount Kenya, from which burst Moi's clenched fist holding a swagger stick. The hill behind the

> '*Nairobi used to be one of the nastiest capitals in the world: dirty, dusty, squalid and at the same time pretentious, a frontier town whose sprinkling of flashily over-dressed safari visitors, minor film stars and local glamour-types, imitating celluloid white hunters, gave it an air of bogus Hollywood or failed St Tropez. Now it has become one of the most attractive and certainly the most flowery of capitals.*'
> Elspeth Huxley, *Forks and Hope* (1963)

monument offers a tremendous view of the Nairobi skyline.

The two parks stand together beside the Uhuru Highway and separated by Kenyatta Avenue. Open: all hours, but unsafe alone or after dark. Admission free.

Vintage steam engine in the Railway Museum

NAIROBI ENVIRONS

LANGATA (see map, page 56)

The Bomas of Kenya

Slightly disappointing African folk centre. Numerous small tribal villages line the paths, but most are empty and those tribal people present are far more interested in selling souvenirs than in explaining their lifestyle. The demonstrations of traditional African dance in the vast central auditorium are more fun, although all are performed by one professional troupe and the costumes are anything but authentic. *Forest Edge Road, Langata (tel: 891 801). 10km southeast of Nairobi off the Langata road. Open: Monday to Friday, 9am–5pm; weekends, 1pm–6pm. Dance exhibitions at 2.30pm weekdays; 3.30pm weekends; and some evenings. Admission charge.*

Langata Giraffe Centre

The highlight of this delightful conservation and education centre is the head-height platform which allows you eyeball to eyeball contact as you hand-feed a small herd of Rothschild giraffes.

Hand-feeding the Rothschild giraffes is the top attraction in Langata

The centre was set up in 1975 to protect these rare animals whose numbers at the time were down to about 100. There are now around 500. There is a bird sanctuary and nature trail next door. *Gogo Falls Road, Langata (tel: 891 078). 18km southwest of Nairobi. Access off Bogani Road, either via Karen Road or Langata Road. Open: daily, 9am–5pm. Admission charge.*

Nairobi National Park

This was the first of Kenya's many national parks, declared such in 1946, after having served time as a game reserve, Samburu grazing land and a military firing range. The park covers an area of 120sq km between the city and the Athi river. Many of its larger mammals were re-introduced after World War II, but it now boasts some 80 species of mammal, and 500 species of bird. Only elephants are too big and too destructive for the relatively small area. With the Nairobi skyline and planes roaring overhead, some find it too close to civilisation, but it is an excellent introduction to Africa's wildlife. This is also the headquarters of Kenya Wildlife Services. *Langata Road (tel: 891 612). 8km from the city centre. Entrances on Langata Road (Main Gate and Langata Gate) and the Airport Road (East Gate). Open: daily, 6am–6pm. Early morning and evening game-viewing is best. Admission charge.*

Nairobi Safari Walk

This is not a zoo, although it feels like one. There is a wide variety of animals including some rare and elusive species such as pygmy hippos, cheetahs and leopards. Funded by Dutch school children, this animal orphanage is now maintained by the World Wide Fund for Nature as an animal hospital and a

NAIROBI ENVIRONS

research and breeding centre for rare species. There are regular audio-visual presentations and films at the weekend. *Langata Road (tel: 891 612). 8km southwest of Nairobi, beside the Main Gate of the national park. Open: daily, 8am–5.30pm. Admission charge.*

Ostrich Park

This is populated by birds of all ages, from balls of fluff to tourist-hardened veterans. None has its head in the sand searching for tasty morsels, accepting titbits from tourists is much easier. There are also excellent craft workshops here. *Near the Giraffe Centre, Langata Road (tel: 891 051). Open: daily, 9am–6pm. Admission charge*

Uhuru Gardens

On this spot, on 12 December 1963, Kenya received its independence from Britain. The Uhuru (freedom) monument was built in 1983 to mark the 20th anniversary of the event. It is an elegant 24m-high spire under which clasped hands of friendship release a dove of peace. On the plinth, freedom fighters recall the nationalist struggle. The gardens in front of the monument are laid out as the map of Kenya. Opposite, a musical fountain was built in 1988 to mark the 25th anniversary of Kenya's independence. *Langata Road. 7km south of the city, just past Wilson Airport. Open: all hours. Admission free.*

The tumbling, muddy waters of the Athi river at the Chania Falls, Thika

LIMURU

Set high on the rim of the Rift Valley, Limuru is one of those odd, charming, colonial hangovers that seem more English than England. Now it is most famous as the headquarters of the ubiquitous Bata Shoes. All around are tightly terraced Kikuyu farms and pine, coffee and tea plantations. In nearby **Tigoni** are the **Kentmere Club**, one of the least spoilt of the old colonial country clubs, **Kiambethu Tea Farm**, which can be toured by prior arrangement, and some charming 15m-high waterfalls, best seen from the grounds of the Waterfalls Inn.

On the way back to Nairobi, stop in **Thogoto**, near Kikuyu town, to see the tiny **Church of the Torch**, built by Scottish missionaries in 1898.

Limuru is 30km northwest of Nairobi on the old Naivasha Road. The Kentmere Club (tel: 0154-41053) is just off the main road in Tigoni, clearly signposted. Kiambethu Farm (tel: 0154-40756) is 3km from the Club. Admission charge.

NGONG

Karen Blixen Museum

Karen Blixen (Isak Dinesen) lived in this low, stone house on her 2,428-hectare coffee farm from 1914 to 1931. Today, it is set in formal gardens while the farm itself has become the up-market suburb of Karen, named after the author. Inside the house are a few of her own paintings and photographs, but most of the furniture was left behind by the producers of *Out of Africa*, the film version of her autobiography, along with the clothes worn by Meryl Streep. (See page 57.)

Karen Road (tel: 882 779). 18km southwest of Nairobi via the Ngong Road. Open: daily, 9.30am–6pm. Admission charge.

Ngong Hills

A popular area among colonial settlers, these beautiful, purple hills on the Nairobi skyline were made famous by Karen Blixen, whose lover, Denys Finch-Hatton is buried here. There are public footpaths along the top from where there are wonderful views. Check the security situation before setting out and don't go out alone.

25km southwest of Nairobi. The road is tarred as far as Ngong town. After that, four-wheel drive is advisable in wet weather. Admission charges for the Finch-Hatton Memorial and the summit. See also page 56.

SOUTHERN RIFT VALLEY

Lake Magadi

This southernmost of Kenya's Rift Valley soda lakes (see page 58) is set in ferocious heat 600m above sea level. Although it covers 100sq km, the lake is less than a metre deep. Popular with flamingos and pelicans, it is an important mining centre for salt and soda ash.

Olorgesailie National Park

Discovered by Dr Louis Leakey in 1942, this fine Stone Age site was almost continuously occupied from 200,000 to 150,000BC. There are few visible remnants of the settlement, but a small site museum houses some of its many animal fossils and Stone Age tools.
The monument is 80km and the lake 120km south of Nairobi. Monument open: 9.30am–6pm. Admission charge. Take a four-wheel drive vehicle equipped with spare fuel and water.

THIKA

Elspeth Huxley's flame trees are long gone and today Thika is a dull industrial town. On the outskirts, the 25m-high **Chania Falls** are best seen from the Blue Post Hotel, a fine example of 1900s colonial architecture.

Twenty kilometres east of the town are the **Fourteen Falls**, a 27m-high, horseshoe-shaped cascade on the Athi river. Just beyond them is the **Ol-Doinyo Sabuk National Park**, covering 18sq km around a 2,146m-high extinct volcano. With fabulous views from the top, this is home to a huge variety of birds and large herds of buffalo.
Thika is 30km northeast of Nairobi. Fourteen Falls and the national park are 20km due east of Thika. The park is open 6am–6pm. Admission free. There are security problems, so take local advice.

The dining room of the Karen Blixen Museum, set up as it was when she lived here

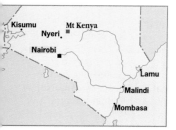

Nairobi City Centre Walk

A contrasting walk through the colourful shopping streets and grand avenues of central Nairobi. For the route, see the Nairobi town plan on pages 44–5. *Allow 1 hour plus shopping time.*

Turn right from the Hilton Hotel on Kimathi Street and cross Moi Avenue to reach the National Archives.

1 THE NATIONAL ARCHIVES

Housed in the neo-classical building directly opposite, the Archives include a public exhibition of photographs and documents from Kenya's history, and a fascinating collection of African tribal art and craft (see page 46).

Walk round the back of the Archives and turn left on to Tom Mboya Street. Then take the second right on to Latema Road and the fourth left on to River Road.

2 TOM MBOYA STREET AND RIVER ROAD

This is the centre of 'African' Nairobi, a colourful blast of loud noise, haphazard stalls and crowded bars that sell everything from whisky to women. It has been made famous by Meja Mwangi's gritty novel, *Going Down River Road*. Sadly, it is also

the most dangerous area of central Nairobi. Take a local guide and leave valuables behind. A lone Westerner is fair game. *Take the second left off River Road, crossing Tom Mboya Street. At the corner with Moi Avenue, on your right, is the old Ismaili Khoja Mosque, which looks more like a Victorian public library. Cross Moi Avenue. Head straight down Biashara Street and turn left into Muindi Mbingu Street, both lined by excellent fabric and batik shops.*

3 CITY MARKET
To your right is the most famous of Nairobi's markets. Although some food and flower stalls still remain, it is now mostly dedicated to crafts.
Continue ahead and turn left on to Banda Street, which leads past the Jamia Mosque and McMillan Library.

4 THE JAMIA MOSQUE
All ornamental gilt and domes, this is the city's main Islamic centre. Tourism is discouraged, but peer through the gates.

5 THE MCMILLAN LIBRARY
This is Nairobi's main library, donated in memory of Sir Northrup McMillan by his widow. McMillan was an Anglicised American knighted for services to the British Empire in World War I.
Turn right in front of the library to come out on to Kenyatta Avenue.

6 KENYATTA AVENUE
The main avenue of colonial Nairobi, this still contains many grand Victorian buildings. To your left are two separate **war memorials** for European and African soldiers. Walk down to your right, past the **African Heritage Centre**

Left: City Market stacked high with flowers and souvenirs

The onion domes of the Jamia Mosque

(see page 150). On your left, at the corner of Koinange Street, is the **Galton-Fenzi Memorial** dedicated to the motoring pioneer and founder of the East African Automobile Association.
Turn left on to Uhuru Highway beside Central Park and Uhuru Park (see page 49). Follow this for three blocks, then turn left on to Harambee Avenue and left again on to Parliament Road.

7 THE PARLIAMENT BUILDING AND KENYATTA MAUSOLEUM
The 1930s Parliament Building is not wildly imposing. In the grounds, ceremonial troops guard the mausoleum of Mzee Jomo Kenyatta (see page 48).
At the roundabout, turn right on to City Hall Way, which runs between the Catholic Holy Family Cathedral and the City Hall on the left, and the Law Courts and the Kenyatta International Conference Centre on the right. Turn left into Wabera Street and take the third left on to Standard Street, a small road lined with craft shops. The Gallery Watatu (see page 46) is on the right. At the junction with Kimathi Street, the famous Thorn Tree Café is on your left. Turn right to return to the Hilton.

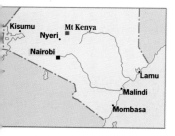

Out of Africa

This tour includes some of Nairobi's most interesting sights. See also pages 50–3. *Allow 1 day. Check security in the Ngong Hills before you set out, and take a local guide.*

Leave Nairobi along the Ngong Road (C60), passing the Commonwealth War Cemetery, the Ngong Race Course, the Ngong Forest and the up-market suburb of Karen. Nine kilometres after Ngong town, the road winds up to the Denys Finch-Hatton Memorial. Ask at the farmhouse for admittance (no set opening hours; admission charge).

1 DENYS FINCH-HATTON MEMORIAL

Denys Finch-Hatton (1887–1931) ran hunting safaris in pre-war Kenya. In 1918, he began a long, tempestuous affair with author Karen Blixen and became an international hero when played by Robert Redford in the film of her autobiography. Finch-Hatton died in a flying accident in 1931.

Continue along the road which winds up into the Ngong Hills for access to the footpath to the summit.

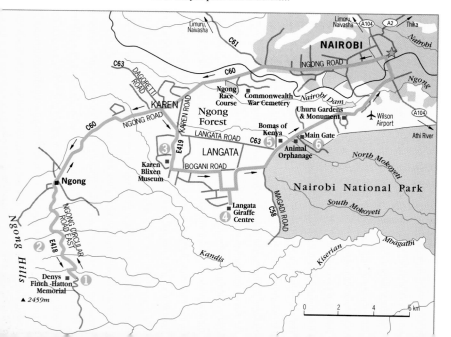

2 THE NGONG HILLS

Legends surround the creation of the sacred Ngong Hills. One claims they were the dirt flicked off God's hands after he had finished creating the world; another that a giant tripped over Mount Kilimanjaro and scraped them from the earth as he fell. Reaching 2,459m high, they form a geographical boundary between the highlands, the Masai plains and the Rift Valley. There are superb views from the top.

Head back along the same road into Karen and turn right, and right again on to Karen Road for the Karen Blixen Museum.

3 THE KAREN BLIXEN MUSEUM

Born in Rungsted, Denmark, in 1885, Karen Blixen arrived in Kenya in 1914 to marry a Swedish cousin, Baron Bror Blixen-Finecke. He soon abandoned the coffee farm she loved so passionately and became a big-game hunter. In 1925, the couple divorced amicably. Constantly beset by troubles ranging from unsuitable soil to syphilis, things came to a head in 1931, when Karen's long-term lover, Denys Finch-Hatton, was killed and she found herself on the brink of bankruptcy. She returned to Denmark where she remained until she died in 1962, writing nine books, including *Out of Africa*, under the pen-name of Isak Dinesen.

Turn right from the museum, then left on to Bogani Road, and right again to follow the signs to the Langata Giraffe Centre.

4 LANGATA GIRAFFE CENTRE

They have huge, soulful eyes, lashes a starlet would kill for and long, gentle black tongues. Although primarily a children's education centre, the most hardened adult will melt when a **Rothschild giraffe** feeds gently from their hand. Follow this by a stroll through the bird sanctuary.

Turn back to Bogani Road, turn right and then left on to Langata Road. The Bomas of Kenya are well signed on the left.

5 THE BOMAS OF KENYA

Stroll under the eucalyptus trees through some 17 different tribal mock-up villages while eager people try to sell you everything from beads to soapstone rhinos. The regular dance performances are an energetic display of shrill song, drums, bright costumes and acrobatics.

One kilometre further on, heading towards the city, are the Main Gate of Nairobi National Park and the Nairobi Safari Walk.

6 NAIROBI NATIONAL PARK AND SAFARI WALK

Silhouetted against a skyscraper skyline, this 120sq km national park is home to everything from black rhinos to zebras. The animal orphanage (the Nairobi Safari Walk) houses a constantly changing array of animals including chimpanzees and, incongruously, tigers from India.

Continue back towards the city past the Uhuru Monument, Wilson Airport, and Nairobi Dam to the walk's start point

The Uhuru (freedom) monument, Langata

The Rift Valley

*A*bout 500 million years ago, there rose across Africa a vast mountain range that stretched north from the Zambezi Valley for nearly 6,000km to the River Jordan. Gradually it eroded away and as the earth's crust weakened, some 70 million years ago, lava bulged upwards on either side. About 20 million years ago, the central ground tore itself apart, creating a jagged rift, thousands of kilometres long, across the face of the continent. The land on either side erupted in a series of volcanic explosions creating great mountains, while the valley floor bubbled and steamed, gradually sinking into a low flat plain, punctuated by volcanoes. This is the Great Rift Valley, one of the greatest geological phenomena on the planet. It was first recognised and named in 1893 by the young Scottish explorer, John Walter Gregory.

The valley today

Punctuated by a long line of lakes, the present-day Rift Valley varies from uninhabitable desert to rich farmland. The majority of its volcanoes have been extinct for at least 2 million years, although many still have clearly defined craters on the summit. Nevertheless, subterranean rumbling continues and there are known to be some 30 active or semi-active volcanoes and many hot springs along its length.

The Rift Valley is at its narrowest just north of Nairobi, a fact clearly visible in the stretch between the Mau Escarpment and the Aberdares. It is about 45km wide here, while the floor ranges from

The view over the Rift Valley floor from the Nyambeni Hills

RIFT VALLEY AND CENTRAL HIGHLANDS

some 500m to 1,600m above sea level. Its walls, sometimes barely visible, climb elsewhere to over 4,000m high, with great slabs of broken rock sliding into the valley floor.

The area contains several lakes, volcanoes and small game parks, and is heavily cultivated by both large-scale European farms and Kalenjin subsistence farms. As President Moi's parliamentary constituency is in the vicinity of Lake Baringo, there is an excellent tarred road running the whole way from Nairobi.

RIFT VALLEY VIEWS

The Rift Valley is so staggeringly vast that it can be difficult to appreciate its size. The small planes that fly across the valley to the Masai Mara give a superb view, but it is clearly visible even from the high-flying, international planes. By road, there are excellent viewing points just north of Limuru on the main Naivasha road, and from the top of the Mau Escarpment on the Kericho road.

Fishing canoe on the freshwater lake at Baringo

KARIANDUSI

Discovered by Louis Leakey in 1928, the Kariandusi Stone Age site was occupied around 10,000 years ago. There are guided tours of the uninspiring excavations and a small museum. The area is dominated by the massive diatomite mine next door. Diatomite is a chalky white material composed of microscopic marine fossils, which is used in brewing, in water filters and as an agricultural insecticide. Opposite, the small Church of Goodwill was modelled on a mission church in Zanzibar in 1949 by Nell Cole as a memorial for her husband, Galbraith, one of the great farming pioneers.

Old Nyahururu road, just south of Lake Elementeita. The prehistoric site and museum are open: daily, 8am–6pm. Admission charge.

LAKE BARINGO

Baringo, the most northerly in a chain of lakes, is a large and beautiful expanse of fresh water, tucked under the high, eastern walls of the valley. A popular tourist stop, it is a superb centre for bird-watching, with over 450 species recorded. It is worth getting up at the crack to join the dawn chorus. You will see almost everything, including the great African fish eagle and, since Lake Nakuru has been virtually dry, the great pink clouds of flamingos. Hippos roam the gardens at night, crocodiles bask in the shallows and monitor lizards sun themselves on the rocky shores.

The **Lake Baringo Club** offers boat trips, bird-watching walks guided by an ornithologist, camel rides, and some watersports, although with crocodiles around, this may not be such a good idea. The club also runs the up-market Island Camp on a small volcanic island and can arrange trips to the local Njemps tribal village and a nearby snake park.

The lake and club are just off the main Rift Valley road, 118km north of Nakuru. Reservations for the club via Block Hotels (see page 171) or Let's Go Travel Ltd (see page 189).

LAKE BOGORIA

This long, skinny soda lake lies at the foot of the looming, black, 600m-high cliffs of the Laikipia Escarpment. It used to be named after Bishop Hannington, who was murdered in 1885 by Buganda tribesmen.

Bogoria does have flamingos and pelicans, and the 107sq km national park also houses one of Kenya's few herds of greater kudu. Yet the sheer peace and overwhelming physical beauty of the setting outweigh even these considerations. Towards the southern end of the lake are a series of dramatic hot springs with bubbling geysers, steaming streams and boiling pools, surrounded by richly patterned lichen-covered rocks. Be very careful when walking around.

Turn off the main road at Marigat, 20km south of Baringo, and follow the signs for 30km through Logumukum village to the park gate. Open: daily, 6am–6pm. Admission charge.

LAKE ELEMENTEITA

As recently as 12,000 years ago, this was part of one huge freshwater lake that also included Lake Nakuru. More recently, it was part of Soysambu, the vast ranch owned by Lord Delamere, one of the most influential of the early settlers. Today, Elementeita is a soda lake, which has some flamingos, but is largely ignored in favour of its larger neighbour, Lake Nakuru.

37km south of Nakuru. Access free at all times.

SODA LAKES

With the movement of the earth's crust in the Rift Valley, many of the lakes have lost their outlets, while sodium carbonate has bubbled up through underground faults. The result is that many of the Rift lakes have become shallow, brackish pans that evaporate into the atmosphere. There are still some hardy fish, but the only life that really flourishes here is microscopic algae and minute crustaceans. These, in turn, are the favourite food of numerous birds, and the soda lakes are superbly suited to the massive flocks of flamingos that crowd their shores.

Hot springs at Lake Bogoria

Fischer's Tower, guarding the entrance to the Njorowa Gorge, Hell's Gate National Park

LAKE NAIVASHA AND ENVIRONS

Naivasha is the largest freshwater lake along the Kenyan section of the Rift Valley, constantly ebbing and flowing, but currently covering about 110sq km. Its name is a corruption of the local word *En-aiposha*, which means 'the lake'!

This was among the first areas to be settled by the colonists. Nearby Wanhoji Valley, on the western slopes of the Aberdares, is the original **Happy Valley**, a notorious spot given its nickname because of the large number of high society, fast-living colonials who lived life to excess here in the 1930s. Down on the lake shore stands a house called Oserian (or the Djinn Palace) which became the centre of their revelries. It is still privately owned and is not open to the public. From 1937 to 1950, Naivasha served as Nairobi airport, with Imperial Airways and BOAC flying boats taking four days for the journey from England.

Today, much of the area is still intensively farmed and is particularly famous for cut flowers, strawberries, and Kenya's only home-grown, drinkable wines. The lake is also a popular holiday playground for Nairobi and a superb centre for bird-watching, with over 400 species catalogued.

The turn-off for South Lake Road is in Naivasha town, 84km northwest of Nairobi. The road continues right around the lake, but the north and west sections are almost impassable.

Crater Lake Game Sanctuary

This privately owned game sanctuary, surrounding a pretty lake in a volcanic crater, covers part of the former 107,245 hectare Ndabibi estate of eccentric pioneer farmer, Gilbert Colville. It later belonged to the notorious Lady Diana Delamere. The wife of Sir Delves Broughton, she had a rampant affair with Josslyn Hay, Earl of Erroll, whose unexplained murder was the subject of the book and film, *White Mischief*. Broughton later committed suicide after he had been tried and acquitted for Erroll's murder, and Diana married Gilbert Colville. Although she later divorced him to marry Lord Delamere, Colville left her his entire estate.

The game-viewing here is nothing particularly special, but there are some pleasant walks beside the lake, a tented camp and ox-wagon safaris.

Follow South Lake Road round to the western shore of Lake Naivasha. The entrance is about 7km beyond the end of the tarmac at Kongoni village. Open: daily, 6am–6pm. Admission charge.

Elsamere

Joy and George Adamson bought this house in 1967 and lived here while struggling to return their pet lioness, Elsa, to the wild. It was here that Joy wrote her world-famous account of their efforts, _Born Free_. After her murder in Shaba National Park in 1980, the house was turned into a small museum and conservation centre. George was also murdered, in 1989, in Kora National Park.

South Lake Road, Naivasha, opposite the Olkaria Geothermal Power Station. Open: daily, 3pm–6pm. Admission charge (includes a film show and hefty afternoon tea).

Elsamere, Joy and George Adamson's home turned into a museum

Hell's Gate National Park

The dramatic Njorowa Gorge, the ancient outlet from Lake Naivasha, has long since dried up, leaving a stark passageway between sheer, red, crumbling cliffs. Since the 1980s, it has been enclosed as part of a 68sq km national park, one of a handful which allow you to walk unguided.

At the entrance to the gorge stands a craggy 25m-tall needle of rock called **Fischer's Tower**, after Gustav Fischer, who explored the area for the Hamburg Geographical Society in 1883. It is home to a large colony of rock hyraxes.

The loop between the two main gates is 22km long, but there is a shorter, 6km (there-and-back) nature trail from the Interpretation Centre. The western end of the gorge comes out into the vast **Olkaria geothermal electricity station.**

South Lake Road, Naivasha (tel: 20510). Open: daily, 6am–6pm. Admission charge. No large predators.

Lake Nakuru, almost solid with thousands
and thousands of flamingos

LAKE NAKURU AND ENVIRONS

Set beneath the high cliffs of the eastern
Rift, Nakuru is a soda lake (see page 61)
which constantly changes size and depth,
depending on the seasonal rains. In the
worst droughts, such as early 1996, it
may dry completely into a shimmer-white
salt pan! An area of 188sq km around the
lake is fenced in as a national park and
sanctuary for Rothschild giraffes and
black rhinos. Nakuru is also one of the
best bird-watching centres in the whole of
Kenya, with a truly fantastic array of
some 450 different species recorded.

When conditions are right, with
sufficient water to support life without
diluting salinity, the lake is home to one
of Kenya's greatest visual experiences –
the shimmering coral glow of up to 2
million flamingos pecking their way
across the shallows. At other times, the
fickle birds gather at other local lakes.

Once down on the mudflats, you are
hit by the full impact of this noisy,
squabbling and smelly colony of greater
and lesser flamingos and pelicans.
Occasionally, if alarmed, they all take to
the air in a cloud of beating salmon
wings. It is a sight never to be forgotten.
Remember to drive up to Baboon Rocks
for the spectacular viewpoint.
*The park entrance is 6km from Nakuru town,
158km northwest of Nairobi (tel: 41605).
Open: daily, 6am–6pm. Admission charge.*

Hyrax Hill

Discovered by the Leakeys in 1926, this
is a major Neolithic and Iron Age site,
occupied from about 3000BC to AD300.
The small museum includes finds from
various nearby excavations. The main
site is a walled hill-fort on a spur with
fine views across Lake Nakuru. There are
few obvious physical remains and those
with a serious interest should buy the
excellent small guidebook.
*Turn off the main road, about 3km south of
Nakuru town. Open: daily, 8am–6pm.
Admission charge.*

Menengai Crater

The second largest surviving volcanic
crater in the world, Menengai's highest
point is 2,242m above sea level. The
crater is several kilometres in diameter
and plunges 483m down from the rim.
The mountain is surrounded by a 60sq
km nature reserve. It is possible to drive
or walk the 8km from the main road to
the summit, and the view from the top is
superb. Security is uncertain, so check
on the situation before setting out.
*The Menengai approach road turns off the
Nyahururu road, just south of Nakuru town.*

MOUNT LONGONOT

At 2,886m, this is the highest of the great
Rift volcanoes. Part of a 52sq km
national park, its almost perfect circular
crater, about 1km in diameter, is clearly
visible from the main Rift viewpoint. The
crater floor is flat, with its own rich eco-
system and steam gushing from crevices.

The cone of Mount Longonot, one of the Rift's largest and youngest volcanoes

Funnels of lava on the slopes have given the mountain its local name, Oloonong'ot (the mountain of steep ridges). Allow up to six hours for the steep climb up from the ranger station and round the circumference of the rim. *60km northwest of Nairobi. Access is via the old Naivasha road, which turns off the new road just north of Limuru. Open: daily, 6am–6pm. Admission charge.*

NYAHURURU

The small, sleepy market town of Nyahururu (the place where the waters run deep) is one of the highest settlements in Kenya (2,360m), and was founded with the arrival of the railway in 1929. The main reason for stopping is the 72m-high **Thomson's Falls**, on the Ewaso Narok river.

In 1883, the British explorer Joseph Thomson named these falls after his father during his epic trek across the Central Highlands and the Rift Valley to Mount Elgon. He then looped back past Lake Victoria and across the southern plains.

The falls, which thunder into a rainbow sprayed gorge beside the Thomson Falls Lodge, are sadly surrounded by hordes of souvenir sellers. There is a crumbling and slippery path to the bottom. If you do walk down, take great care.
50km from Nakuru on the northern end of the Aberdares. Admission free at any time.

THE WHITE TRIBE

There is an image of the Kenyan settlers as hard-living high society misfits who spent their days stalking defenceless elephants and their nights bed-hopping. Among the early settlers, there was a surprising number of old school ties, and by the 1930s, the lifestyle of the upper-crust Happy Valley Set had become notorious. The majority of the country's white population was a very different breed, however. Hard-working farmers and administrators, many arrived after the First and Second World Wars as part of a government soldier-settler scheme, which gave cheap land to its war heroes. The early life was anything but comfortable as they forced the land into production almost by sheer willpower, living in shacks, dying of fever, and often going bankrupt.

In the run-up to independence, the white population dwindled rapidly. These days, there are only about 10,000 permanent residents. Many are still on the land; others are in the tourist industry, white hunters who simply swapped their guns for cameras. They have a comfortable life, on the whole, still retaining some of the trappings of the colonial era, such as large houses and servants. Few could be called real racists, but they do tend to cling together, and to the past, and mix relatively little. They all love the country with a passion but, aware of their delicate position, they keep their heads down, hoping to be ignored – a tiny, privileged minority who are tolerated but not liked.

Left: White Kenyans are a minority now, but are still passionately devoted to their land

The other 45,000 or so white people in the country are a different breed altogether, a floating population of expatriates and aid workers known as 'two-year wonders'. Some throw themselves into the 'African experience' with a vengeance; others live a ghetto-like existence, trying to pretend they have never left home. The Africans welcome the money they bring, but are bemused and amused by them all.

Below: the verandah of the Manor Hotel, Mombasa, a favourite watering-hole of the white tribe

The Central Highlands

'Looking back on a sojourn in the African highlands, you are struck by your feeling of having lived for a time up in the air... Up in this high air you breathed easily, drawing in a vital assurance and lightness of heart. In the highlands, you woke up in the morning and thought: Here I am, where I ought to be.'
Karen Blixen, *Out of Africa* (1937).

Most people who have ever lived in the Central Highlands think them perfect. The Kikuyus regard the area as sacred land, given to them by God. The settlers looked at the rich earth, the tumbling mountain streams, felt the cool rush of the wind and found a farmers' paradise. Most of the habitable land is between 1,800m and 3,000m above sea level, and almost everything can grow here, from tea and coffee, pine and eucalyptus on the higher slopes to maize and oranges, pineapples and bananas on the lower. The Highlands are said to have one of the most perfect climates in the world, with just enough rain, warm days and crisp, cool nights. They are even free of

many tropical diseases that blight the lower lands.

These days, few of the huge colonial estates remain, but those that do are quite spectacularly large, such as the massive Del Monte pineapple plantation, said to grow nearly a third of the world's pineapples. Most of the estates' lands have been returned to the Kikuyu people and carved up into intensively cultivated subsistence plots. Wherever you look the scenery is a rich tapestry of steep terraces that carpet the hillsides in glowing green. Yet, however beautiful these are, the Highlands' crowning glories are its great mountains, the wild Aberdares and the cloud-covered, snow-capped summit of Mount Kenya.

THE ABERDARES

Formed by volcanic lava welling up through great fissures in the earth, the Aberdares are dramatically beautiful mountains, whose peak, Ol-Doinyo Lesatima (3,999m), is the third highest in Kenya. The range runs roughly north to south, for about 60km. Known to the Kikuyu as Nyandarua ('Drying Hide'), because of their resemblance to a skin over a drying frame, they were renamed in 1884 by Joseph Thomson, the first European to see them, after Lord Aberdare, president of the Royal Geographical Society. In 1950, a 767sq km national park was created.

A little slice of home, England recreated at the Aberdare Country Club

Dawn over Mount Kenya, from the Aberdare Forest

Several bands of distinctive vegetation wrap the mountains, from Tarzan-style jungle, through dense bamboo forest to the weird alpine plants of the high moorlands. The lower slopes support a wide variety of animal life, from elephant, rhino and buffalo, to some rare species, such as the enchanting, chestnut-coated bongo antelope. However, the animals are too timid and the vegetation too thick for good game-viewing. (See the map on page 80, **Aberdare Mountain Drive**.)

ABERDARE COUNTRY CLUB

An attractive corner of little England, this doubles as the local country club and a popular tourist hotel. Built on a precipitous slope, it has lovely gardens and superb views. The grounds also include a small game sanctuary and a golf course. Activities include walking,

tennis, swimming, riding and fishing. *Mweiga, 10km north of Nyeri. PO Box 449, Nyeri (tel: 0171-55620 or fax: 0171-55224). Booking via Lonrho (see page 171). Daily membership available for non-residents.*

THE ARK

Built in the shape of an ark, this hotel is designed for close-up sedentary game-viewing, with viewing platforms, a photographic bunker and floodlights powerful enough for night pictures. Situated in the Salient area on the western slopes of the Aberdares, it stands beside a large, swampy waterhole and artificial salt-lick, surrounded by dense forest and cavernous valleys. *No access for private vehicles. Guests are picked up daily at 2.30pm from the Aberdare Country Club, which also handles bookings.*

Buffalo are frequent visitors to the Treetops waterhole

TREETOPS

The original and most famous of the 'treetop' hotels, first inspired by Peter Pan and opened literally as a two-room tree-house in 1932. It was here, in 1952, that Princess Elizabeth heard of her father's death and her own accession to the British throne. It is now a much larger hotel, but is still on stilts overlooking a salt-lick and water-hole for comfortable, night-time game-viewing.
No access for private transport. Reservations via Block Hotels (see page 171); lunchtime pick-up from the Outspan Hotel.

MOUNT KENYA AND ENVIRONS

One of the largest single mountains in the world and the second highest in Africa, this snow-capped colossus bestrides the Equator with a base 120km in diameter and its highest peak (Batian) soaring to 5,199m. The mountain, named Kere-Nyaga (literally either Mountain of Whiteness or Mountain like Ostrich Feathers), is said by the Kikuyu to be the home of the gods. The first European to see it was a German missionary, Johann Krapf, in 1849, but his discovery was howled down in disbelief. It was not until Joseph Thomson found the mountain again in 1883 that he was finally vindicated. The great mountain has since given its name to the entire country.

Mount Kenya is a volcanic cone which last erupted about 2 million years ago. Its crater has long since eroded away to leave smoothly curving slopes, while the craggy peaks at the summit are the last remnants of the hard volcanic core. The deep valleys around the summit have been carved out by glaciers. In 1893, 18

ITALIAN MEMORIAL CHURCH

Looking as if it has strayed off a Tuscan hillside, this was built in 1952 by the Italian government as a memorial to the Italian soldiers and prisoners of war who died in Kenya during both world wars. There were several large POW camps in the country, including one at nearby Nyeri. It is a moving sight, the walls lined by hundreds of memorial plaques, many adorned with photos and mementos left by visiting relatives.
Turn left, about 5km north of Nyeri. Open: daily, 8am–5pm. Ask the caretaker to unlock the church. Admission free.

OUTSPAN HOTEL

A charming old colonial hotel with fine views across to Mount Kenya. The grounds contain a fascinating small museum dedicated to Lord Baden-Powell (1857–1941), founder of the Boy Scout movement, who lived in the cottage, Paxtu, from 1938 to 1941. He is buried in the graveyard of St Peter's Church, Nyeri.
Nyeri Road, Nyeri. Reservations via Block Hotels (see page 171). Ask at reception for admission to the museum. Admission charge. St Peter's Church, Aberdares Road (opposite the CalTec Garage). Access to the grave is free.

glaciers were recorded; today there are only seven. They are all retreating rapidly and some say they will have vanished within 25 years.

For information on climbing Mount Kenya, see **Mount Kenya walks**, pages 76–9.

ISIOLO

Isiolo (1,250m) is a hot, dusty town below the dramatic escarpment which plunges down over 2,000m from the Central Highlands. It acts as a gateway to the remote deserts of the northeast, and its population has swelled rapidly with the arrival of thousands of Somali refugees. It has a lawless, frontier town atmosphere, its streets roamed by gangs of wild-eyed youths, high on alcohol or *miraa* (a locally grown narcotic plant). Be very careful of security. If you plan to drive further north, check in with the local police point.

82km north of Nanyuki on the A2 (the Great North Road).

The summit of Mount Kenya is a rare sight, clear for only a few minutes each morning

Visitor petting a baby bongo at the Safari Club Animal Orphanage

LEWA DOWNS

A combination of cattle ranch, private game park and rhino sanctuary, the 16,188-hectare Ranch House offers rich game-viewing (although no lions); comfortable accommodation; a laid-back atmosphere; bush walks, horse rides, day and night game-drives and birdwatching; and for an additional cost, sightseeing flights over Mount Kenya. Alternative accommodation is available at the nearby luxury Lerai Tented Camp.
PO Box 14398, Isiolo. The entrance to the farm is about 20km past the Meru fork on the Isiolo road. Booking via Bush Homes (see page 189), Lerai (tel: 331 191; fax: 330 698).

MOUNT KENYA SAFARI CLUB

An extraordinary oasis of unashamed luxury, this is one of the finest hotels in the world. Although the original house was built in the 1930s, it was the American film star, William Holden, who turned it into this Hollywood dream, with a visitors' book that reads like *Who's Who*. There are 40 hectares of impeccably manicured gardens roamed by peacocks and sacred ibis, a golf course, a tennis court that crosses the Equator, and a 405-hectare private game-ranch.

Animal Orphanage

This delightful institution is run by the William Holden Foundation as a conservation and education centre. It is possible to spend hours playing with baby bongos, kept here as part of a captive breeding programme, tickling the giant tortoises and cuddling the bush babies. Entrancing for adults, it is an essential stop for children.
PO Box 35, Nanyuki (tel: 22960 or fax: 22754). Booking via Lonrho (see page 171). Turn right near the Nanyuki Equator sign. Accommodation expensive. Day membership available, plus separate entry fee for the Animal Orphanage.

MERU

Founded originally as a centre for hardwood timber (the Meru Oak), Meru is now famous for potatoes and *miraa*. Known in the Middle East as *q'at*, the twigs of the *miraa* bush are a narcotic, perfectly legal in Kenya, which produces a high that can lead to severe sleep deprivation if overdone.

Meru National Museum

A tiny, faded museum in the old District Commissioner's Office with interesting displays about the Meru tribe, a reconstructed village, gardens growing local medicinal herbs, and a horrific little snake park and zoo.
Northeast corner of the Mount Kenya ring road. The museum is just past the town hall. Open: Monday to Saturday, 9.30am–6pm; Sunday, 11am–6pm. Admission charge.

African Nativity in Murang'a Cathedral, a memorial to Mau Mau victims

MURANG'A

The Cathedral Church of St James and All Martyrs, Murang'a, was consecrated by the Archbishop of Canterbury in 1955 as a memorial to the many Christians who refused to take the blood-curdling oath of loyalty demanded by the Mau Mau independence guerrillas and were killed as a result. Inside is a series of murals translating the story of the Nativity to an African setting painted by leading Kenyan artist, Elimo Njau. He now runs the Payapaa Art Centre (see page 48).

87km north of Nairobi at the foot of the Mount Kenya ring road. The cathedral is on a hill above the town centre. Ask the caretaker to unlock the building. Admission free.

NANYUKI

A charming market-town with tree-lined streets, Nanyuki has many old-fashioned colonial shops, of which the Settler

Store, built in 1938, is the most famous. There is a large and lively market, and a Spinners' and Weavers' Cooperative, where you can watch the women working the local wool and buy a variety of rugs, shawls and jumpers.

South of the town, at the big Equator sign, crowds of souvenir sellers try to demonstrate how water swirls down the plug in different directions in the northern and southern hemispheres.

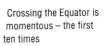

On the Mount Kenya ring road. The Weavers' Cooperative is in the grounds of the Presbyterian Church, Nyeri Road. Open: Monday to Friday, 9am–5pm; Saturday, 9am–12.30pm. Admission free.

Crossing the Equator is momentous – the first ten times

THE KIKUYU

According to legend, Mogai (God), who lives on Kere-Nyaga (Mount Kenya), gave the Central Highlands to Gikuyu, founder of the Kikuyu tribe. Gikuyu settled

From them sprang the nine clans of the tribe. To this day, Kikuyu people build their houses facing sacred Mount Kenya.

The Kikuyu are a Bantu tribe, who settled in the area in the 16th century. Four hundred years later, the early settlers fixed their sights on this lush region. Blind to the complex system of land ownership at the very heart of Kikuyu civilisation, they saw only vast tracts of 'virgin' bush and failed to realise that every centimetre had an owner and was used in some way. They saw simple homes with an

happily and over the years had nine daughters, but no sons. So he went to Mogai for help and Mogai created nine men to be their husbands.

Kikuyu ceremonial dress is highly
colourful and dramatic.
Sadly, western clothes are far
more common these days

oral tradition and assumed these
were a primitive and stupid people.
They saw smiles and failed to see the
bitter resentment of the dispossessed.
Winston Churchill described them as
'light-hearted, tractable, if brutish
children'. Almost to a man, the
settlers misunderstood the Kikuyu
culture.

On their part, the Kikuyu soaked
up the missionaries' education, many
converting to Christianity, and adapted
easily to Western ways. Then they
began to try and retrieve their stolen
lands, first by founding nationalist
organisations which sent emissaries to
London, then resorting to the terror of
Mau Mau (see **History**, pages 8–9). At
independence, they claimed the
government of Kenya.

Today, the tribe numbers nearly 7
million, most of whom still live amid the
tight patchwork of terraced fields on the
Highland slopes. Many have also
adapted with glee to big business and
city living. They are not, at present, in
control of the government, but they are
still the single most powerful financial
and political force in Kenya.

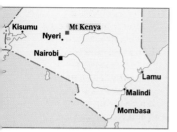

Hiking up Mount Kenya

Mount Kenya has long, smooth slopes on three sides, and the climb to the ring of rocky peaks at the summit can be made by anyone of average fitness. The result of this accessibility is that numerous untrained and over eager people, who have never before been at high altitude, behave without any regard for their surroundings and several of them die on the mountain every year. Act sensibly, however, and even if you come back dog tired, wet and uncomfortable, it will be one of the greatest triumphs of your life.

THE ROUTES

There are eight accepted routes up the mountain, of which three are climbed regularly; Naro Moru to the west (the easiest and most popular, see pages 78–9); Sirimon to the north; and Chogoria to the east. The actual summit is Batian, at 5,199m, but to get there involves crossing the glaciers and some real mountaineering. The amateur treks all aim for Point Lenana, the third highest peak at 4,985m.

It is possible to do either a circular walk around the peaks or to come back down a different route, but the latter alternative should only be attempted by the very fit and experienced.

STAYING HEALTHY

There are two main health hazards on the mountain. The first is altitude sickness, which can strike anyone, no matter how young or fit, and in its acute form can kill. This is caused by climbing too fast and the temptations are enormous on these short and relatively easy routes. The climb can be accomplished in two to three days but, to be sure that you give yourself time to acclimatise, allow five. If you feel nauseated, over-exhausted or have a severe headache, stop at once. If the symptoms get worse, head down hill immediately.

The second hazard is hypothermia, a condition caused by getting too cold and run down. The best way to avoid it is to keep warm and try not to get wet or exhausted.

Three rocky peaks, the last remnants of the mountain's volcanic cone, crown the snow-capped summit of Mount Kenya – Batian, Nelion, and Lenana. The last peak is the most accessible and the target for most climbers

SUPPLIES AND PORTERAGE

For safety reasons, you are not allowed to climb solo. There are organised tours, but if you want a little independence, hire a full set of mountain equipment and a guide and/or porter at affordable rates.

You will need warm, wind-proof clothing, gloves, stout walking-boots and plenty of socks, a good tent and sleeping bag, a stove and lots of high-energy food and drinks. Also take high UV-protection sunglasses, a hat and sunblock.

Naro Moru River Lodge

A comfortable hotel whose mountain shop hires out all equipment needed, and handles bookings for the mountain huts. Naro Moru town is also the headquarters of the Mountain National Parks and the Guides and Porters Association.
PO Box 18, Naro Moru (tel: 0176-62622 or fax: 0176-62211).

Mountain Rock Lodge

The lodge will organise everything but equipment for you.
PO Box 333, Nanyuki (tel: 0176-62625/98).

Tropical Ice and Bike Treks

Two of several companies offering all-in organised climbs. Tropical Ice caters for more experienced climbers.
Tropical Ice, PO Box 57341, Nairobi (tel: 740 811 or fax: 740 826); Bike Treks, see page 143.

FURTHER INFORMATION
Mount Kenya Map

By Andrew Wielochowski and Mark Savage; 1:50,000 map with excellent detailed notes on the routes.
The Mountain Club of Kenya
PO Box 45741, Nairobi (tel: 501 747). Mount Kenya National Park, PO Box 69, Naro Moru (tel: 0171-2383).

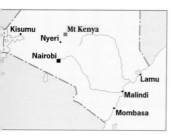

Mount Kenya, the Naro Moru Route

Mount Kenya is one of only a handful of great mountains whose summit is accessible to non-climbers. The Naro Moru route is the easiest ascent, but you still need to be fit and properly equipped. For more practical details, see pages 76–7. *Allow up to 5 days.*

Start at the Naro Moru River Lodge, 35km north of Nyeri on the Mount Kenya ring road.

THE LODGE TO THE GATE

This first 17km stretch of the walk is all on roads and it is

possible to hire a vehicle for the journey, unless you wish to break yourself in with some relatively easy walking. The road leads through Naro Moru town, then turns right to start the climb through farmland. After 12km, you enter thick forest. As you near the gate, this turns into conifer forest and the last short section opens out again beside the park's airstrip.

THE GATE TO THE MET STATION

The summit of Mount Kenya is a national park. You must pay your entry fees at the gate (2,400m). If it has been raining, this is the last point accessible by vehicle; in good weather a four-wheel drive vehicle can get as far as the Met Station. About 1km beyond the gate, you enter the thick tropical bamboo forest. After 7km, the Percival Bridge crosses a deep ravine and 3km further on, you reach the Meteorological Station at 3,000m, the first overnight stop.

MET STATION TO MACKINDER'S CAMP

This stage covers 12km, climbs 1,150m and takes 6–7 hours. About 40 minutes after leaving the Met Station, the forest ends abruptly and you come out on to open moorland, with superb views (on good days) across the Aberdares and the Nyeri Valley. The next section, which takes about three hours, is known as the Vertical Bog – horribly soggy after rain, but not too bad in dry weather. Red and white markers show the path.

From now on, keep an eye open for the extraordinary moorland plants, such as giant groundsel, lobelias and heather.

Left: turquoise melt water glows in the tarn on the Lewis Glacier, Mount Kenya

As you come out on to the ridge above the Teleki Valley, you should get your first clear view of the peaks. There are two routes across the valley; short(ish) and sharp on the left, and longer and easier on the right. They join up on the far side for the last climb to Mackinders Camp and the Teleki Hut, at 4,200m. Spend two nights here acclimatising.

TO POINT LENANA

The summit only peers out of the clouds for a few short minutes early every morning, so if you wish to make the summit in one bite, and see the view, your day starts horribly early – around 3am! There is a climb of about 800m (three to four hours) to the top. Take the main path past the Ranger Station and after 0.5km, take the right-hand fork. This leads over another stretch of boggy ground around the head of the valley and up a large scree slope. At the top of the ridge, there are superb views of the Lewis Glacier and the southeast face of Point Nelion. From here, the path crosses a rocky plateau before climbing up more scree to the Austrian Hut at 4,790m. If taking five days, this is your last night's stop. From the hut, the last 200m to the summit are straight up.

The journey down can be done in a single day.

First stop, the Met Station

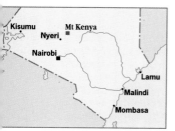

Aberdare Mountain Drive

This route crosses the southern section of the Aberdares, reaching a height of 3,500m and passing through some of Kenya's most spectacular scenery, with rich farmland, bamboo forest and Alpine moorland. The road is the best in the National Park (tel: 0170-55024), but even so it should not be attempted except in a four-wheel drive vehicle, and is often closed completely after heavy rain. *Allow 1 day.*

Start the drive from Nyeri town. Take the Nyahururu road north for approximately 5km and then turn left on to the road signposted to the Ruhuruini Gate and the Aberdare National Park. This leads past the Italian Memorial Church (see also page 70) to reach Ihururu village. Turn right at the village, clearly signed to Kimathi Secondary School. Fork right at each new turn after this. The gate is signed, but the notices are not always easy to spot.

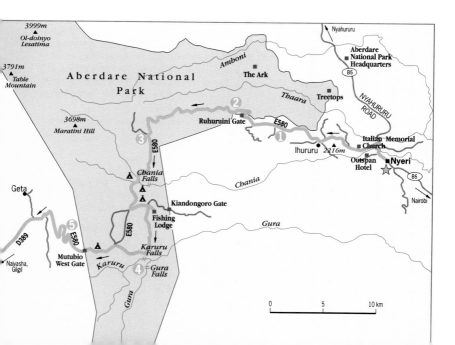

1 THE APPROACH ROAD

The road is magnificent, climbing steadily through rich farmland, with wide vistas over countless small maize plots ringed by banana trees and huge open fields of velvet smooth tea, broken by patches of eucalyptus and pine.

At the edge of the forest reserve, hoot for the gate-keeper to open the barrier.

2 THE FOREST BELT

Six kilometres further on, Ruhuruini Gate is tucked into a secluded valley surrounded by vast stands of high bamboo. Once through the gate, the road winds ever more steeply around tight bends in the mountainside, with sharp falls and dramatic views over cavernous steep-sided valleys. It is impossible to see far into the dense undergrowth, but even the roadside displays a fantastic tapestry of gnarled trees dripping with Spanish moss, bamboo and wild flowers. Keep an eye open for animals, from buffalo to the timid bongo, or elegant troops of black-and-white colobus monkeys in the high branches.

As you reach the heights, above 3,000m, you come out on to the open moorlands. Shortly afterwards, the road forks. Turn left.

3 THE MOORLAND

This is the only place in Kenya where the strange, giant alpine vegetation of the high moorlands is accessible by vehicle. It is a stark landscape, cool and often shrouded in mist. A turning to the left, just past the campsites, leads down to the access point for the 25m-high **Chania (Queen's Cave) Waterfall**.

Continue south for about 4km to a crossroads, where you turn left. About 1km on, the second turning on the left leads to the Self-help fishing camp, a simple cabin used

Clearing fallen trees off the road across the Aberdares

as a base by keen trout fishermen. Keep on the main road for another 7km.

4 GURA FALLS

A footpath to the left leads towards the 275m-high **Karuru Falls** and the 300m-high **Gura Falls** (the highest in Kenya), two thin, bright ribbons weaving down into the ravine near the confluence of the Gura and Karuru rivers. You should take a ranger with you if you plan to make the walk (about 6km there and back).

From here, the road turns west to cross the ridge, leading to Mutubio West Gate, still about 3,000m high, and the exit from the national park.

5 RIFT VALLEY DESCENT

The views get even more spectacular to the west, looking out over the forests to the Rift Valley, some 2,000m below. The road hurls itself down the mountain in a series of switchbacks, plunging through the forests and out into farmland near **Wanhoji Valley** (the original 'Happy Valley'). Shortly after this, it joins the main road to Naivasha.

Western Kenya

*T*he Masai Mara is one of Kenya's greatest tourist attractions, visited each year by many thousands. The rest of the rolling plains to the west of the Rift are territories almost untouched by tourism. You will not find luxury lodges or organised safaris, but those prepared to make their own arrangements will find some of the most beautiful scenery the country has to offer.

The plains beyond the Mau Escarpment, which makes up the western wall of the Great Rift Valley, are made up of Kenya's oldest rocks, re-emerging from a lava plain that bears both gold and soapstone (see page 16). In the south, around the Masai Mara, the climate is dry and the vegetation scrubby. Further north, Lake Victoria has created its own micro-climate. Warm and humid with year-round rain, it provides perfect conditions both for the lush natural vegetation and the intensive farming that has laid row upon dense row of narrow terraces across even the steepest hillsides. This is one of the most densely populated corners of the country, home to the Luo and Luyia, two of the largest tribes in Kenya, both of whom have a strong farming tradition.

Lake Victoria dominates the western fringe of the area, but there are many other attractions for the visitor, from the quite staggeringly vast tea plantations of Kericho to the Kakamega Forest Reserve, one of Kenya's last remaining areas of primeval forest and a bird-watcher's paradise. Beyond this, between Kitale and the Uganda border, rears the massive bulk of Mount Elgon, the country's second highest mountain. Four-wheel drive is advisable if you wish to take full advantage of the area.

The densely cultivated fields of the Luyia people, near Kericho

WESTERN KENYA

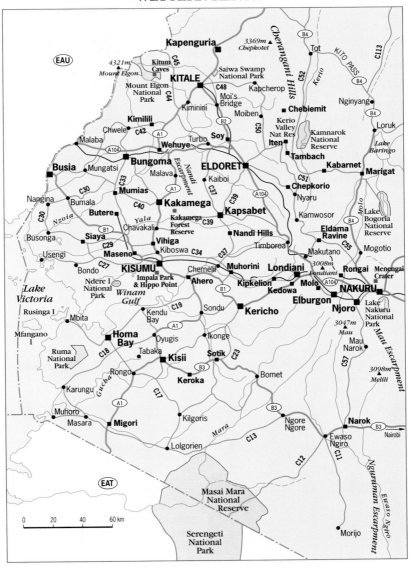

Lions prowling through the golden savannah of the Masai Mara

THE MASAI MARA

The Masai Mara is a name to conjure up romance. This is the northern tip of the great Serengeti plains, separated politically at independence, but still operating as one giant game park. It has a stupendous concentration of game, particularly during the great migration.

Lying between 1,000 and 2,000m in altitude, the reserve covers 1,510sq km, most of which is savannah grassland and acacia scrub. Surrounded by eight conservation areas, there are 3,000

Zebra and wildebeest are usually found together

elephants, so many lions they almost get boring, leopards, cheetahs and even a slowly recovering population of black rhino (37 at the time of writing). Hippos and crocodiles wallow in the rivers and in the skies above wheel several hundred species of bird, from vultures to falcons, hornbills to sunbirds. Above all, the vast, rippling grasslands are home to enormous herds of wildebeest and zebra, antelope and gazelle, buffalo and giraffe, who conveniently crop the grass short enough for perfect game-viewing. It is a safari feast of quite overwhelming proportions.

About 138,000 people visit the park each year, leading purists to claim it is a zoo. It is anything but. The animals are completely unafraid, offering unsurpassed photographic opportunities, but they are still wild, leading a totally natural life. The biggest problem is that over-eager drivers head off across the plains, getting too close to the animals and creating dusty ruts in the fragile grasslands. Sections of the park have to be closed occasionally to allow the

vegetation to re-establish itself.
Meanwhile, the park authorities try to
drum up funding to create proper roads.
Most visitors stay in the more accessible
eastern section of the park. If you wish to
get away, head west, where concentrations
of game are, if anything, even greater.

The Mara is on traditional Masai
grazing land. Several Masai *manyattas*
(villages) near the main gates have set
themselves up as attractions. Pay a flat fee
to the chief and you can wander round,
talk to the villagers, take as many pictures
as you like, and, of course, buy souvenirs.
*In the southwest corner of Kenya, about
250km from Nairobi. The nearest town is
Narok. The best time to visit is between July
and October. Daily admission charge.*

Above: hide at Keekorok Lodge. Below: wildebeest crossing a river during annual migration

THE GREAT MIGRATION

The annual migration of the humble
wildebeest, or gnu, is one of the
greatest wildlife spectacles on earth.
Up to 2 million wildebeest trek north
each year from the Serengeti to the
Masai Mara in search of fresh grazing,
bringing with them some half a million
zebra. They arrive sometime in July
and spend the next three months in the
park, while they and all their
surrounding predators grow fat and
sleek. Towards the end of September
someone, somewhere, blows a
whistle, and suddenly the herds are on
the move again. This is not a casual
drift southwards, but a purposeful
march with endless, almost military
columns steadily tramping off across
the horizon.

The absolute single-mindedness of
the wildebeest is awesome. The weak
are left behind, a mother has only a few
minutes to mourn the loss of a dead calf
before she must swing back into line.
They make no allowance for accidents
and many die at river crossings – if one
slips, the others continue over the top
and the resulting tangle of beasts is
washed downstream. If there is an
obstacle in their way, they will not try to
find a new route round it but will try to
force their way through, or simply stop.
In the parks they are safe but elsewhere
many thousands have died when their
path to water has been blocked by a
rancher's fence.

THE SCARLET WARRIORS

Closely related nomadic tribes, the Masai and Samburu are herders of cattle and goats (many Samburu also keep camels). Physically beautiful, they dress in red with loads of intricate bead jewellery. There is no significance in the colour, they simply like it. They believe in one god, Nkai, but religion is a private affair, and the rites of passage, from the naming of a child to circumcision, are secular ceremonies. Their traditional diet is blood and milk.

The *manyatta* is home to the extended family group, with the husband and each of his wives having separate houses. Girls stay with their mothers until they marry, boys move in with their father at about six. The small boys are in charge of the herds. After circumcision, at between 14 and 17, they become *moranis* (warriors) and move off to live in a separate village. Their traditional pastimes were killing lions or rustling cattle;

today they spend most of their time preening. At about 25, the men become junior elders, and are allowed to marry. Their duties now are counting the herds out and in, and decision-making. All the day to day work, including building houses, is done by the women, who have no rights or say in tribal affairs.

Immensely proud peoples, both tribes have preferred to retain their traditional lifestyle in the

The most colourful, proud and famous of Kenya's many tribes, the Masai still live a largely traditional lifestyle

face of all odds, and only very recently have any succumbed to Western ways or even been to school. Even so, they cling to polygamy, huge families and ever-growing herds, with cattle or camels the only symbol of wealth they recognise. The authorities are actively seeking to make them join the modern world. For the moment, they remain guardians of one of the last great nomadic traditions in Africa.

MOUNT ELGON AND ENVIRONS

The whole Mount Elgon area suffers from heavy rains almost every afternoon, so try and do your sightseeing and complete any journeys on dirt roads in the morning, before you become shrouded in cloud and the roads are rendered impassable.

KAKAMEGA FOREST RESERVE

A 45sq km forest reserve tucked beneath the Nandi Escarpment at around 1,500m, Kakamega is a throw-back to the days when primeval forests covered the length and breadth of Africa. The only remaining section of such forest in East Africa, it has 125 species of massive hardwood trees and literally hundreds of species of birds and animals, many of which are found nowhere else in Kenya. Look out for the brilliantly coloured turacos, colobus and blue monkeys, the bush-tailed porcupine and the scaly-tailed flying squirrel.

Two access roads turn off the Kisumu-Kitale road (A1), about 10km south and 20km north of Kakamega. There is one small rest house, 5km walk from the road at Shinalyu village. Take your own food. Admission free.

KITALE

A sleepy little town with a population of about 30,000, Kitale houses the excellent little **National Museum of Western Kenya**. It was founded in 1972 around the private collection of butterflies, medals and oddities of a local farmer, Colonel Stoneham. Other sections include animal, geological and ethnographic displays, such as a fascinating case on traditional medicines with treatments for bone cancer, nose bleeds and syphilis. Outside, a nature trail leads through a small area of forest, and past some traditional homesteads, crocodile and tortoise pens.

Kisumu Road. Open: daily, 8.30am–6pm. Admission charge.

MOUNT ELGON NATIONAL PARK

This remote and beautiful park covers 169sq km on the eastern slopes of Mount Elgon (the western slopes are in Uganda). A free-standing volcanic cone, the mountain is the second highest in Kenya, at 4,321m. When the weather is clear (in the mornings), the views from the mountain, even from the gate, are magnificent, while the higher slopes are swathed in dense forest, home to bushbuck, buffalo and elephant as well as a host of smaller animals and birds. At the top there is moorland, with giant alpine vegetation (see page 21). The actual summit consists of a ring of rocky peaks surrounding the crater lake.

About 9km from the gate, eroded volcanic ash has formed a series of deep caves. The largest and most accessible (about 0.5km walk from the road) are the **Kitum Caves**, said to have been the inspiration for Rider Haggard's novel, *She*. The caves are natural salt-licks and at night the elephants pick their way up precipitous mountain paths and across the unstable rock falls to gouge the minerals from the walls. It is possible to see the marks made by their tusks, as well as vast colonies of bats. Wear shoes with a good grip and take a powerful flashlight.

Tel: 0325-20329. Chorlim Gate is about 30km west of Kitale. Camping only within the park. Alternatively, stay at the simple lodge just outside, or Lokitela Farm about 18km away (see page 173). Open: daily, 6am–6pm. You will need permission and a ranger with you if walking. Admission charge.

SAIWA SWAMP NATIONAL PARK

This tiny 2sq km park, in the swamplands surrounding the Koitobos river, was set up to preserve the only remaining natural habitat of the Sitatunga antelope in Kenya. Access is on foot only, with a series of walking trails and observation points. There is excellent birdwatching and the remote prospect of seeing a leopard.

5km off the main road, 18km north of Kitale. Open: daily, 6am–6pm. There are no facilities. Admission free.

A giant groundsel that is endemic to the slopes of Mount Elgon

The Luo tribe fish for Nile perch and tilapia in Lake Victoria

LAKE VICTORIA

'...there lay the end of our pilgrimage – a glistening bay of the great Lake surrounded by low shores and shut in to the south by several islands, the whole softly veiled and rendered weirdly indistinct by a dense haze. The view, with arid-looking euphorbia-clad slopes shading gently down to the muddy beach, could not be called picturesque, though it was certainly pleasing.'
Joseph Thomson, *Through Masai Land* (1883)

At 67,483sq km, Lake Victoria is the second largest freshwater lake in the world (only Lake Superior in North America is larger). The first European to sight this vast inland sea was John Hanning Speke in 1858. On little evidence and a strong gut reaction, he declared the lake to be the source of the White Nile, only to be howled down by other explorers. It was 1875 before H M Stanley eventually proved him right.

From then on, the lake attracted intense interest in Europe as the colonial powers dreamed in vain of opening up a navigable route along the Nile to the Mediterranean. Their attempts to reach Uganda across the lake were also responsible for creating the East African Railway and colonising the Kenyan

Highlands (see pages 144–5).

Now officially renamed Nyanza (a name rarely used), the lake acts as a boundary between Tanzania, Uganda and Kenya, which owns only a tiny corner – 3,785sq km. It is remarkable more for its sheer size than its physical beauty, the persistent haze and cloud cover turning its surface a dull steely grey for much of the year. Only a handful of fishing boats and one local ferry (see page 140) ever break the monotony of the scene.

KISUMU

The third largest city in Kenya, with a population of about 160,000, Kisumu was founded in 1901 as the inland railhead of the East African Railway. At the time, it was named Port Florence after Florence Whitehouse, wife of the railway's General Manager, who hammered the last rail into place. Today, it is a friendly, bustling, rather old-fashioned centre with few actual sights. Take the time to wander around, and visit the splendid market at the corner of Nairobi Road and Jomo Kenyatta Highway.

Impala Park and Hippo Point

This 16-hectare game sanctuary and animal orphanage is one of the few homes of the rare sitatunga. Hippo Point, next door, is theoretically the best place for seeing hippos, but they do wander. Both places are excellent spots from which to see Lake Victoria's spectacular sunsets.
Beside the Sunset Hotel, 3km south of the Kisumu. Both are open at all times. Admission free. Check at the hotel about the area's security.

Kisumu Museum

An excellent small museum with some curious oddities, such as a stuffed lion savaging a stuffed wildebeest. Most of it is given over to a fascinating display of local traditional lifestyle and crafts, from musical instruments to a reconstructed Luo village. There are also an aquarium, a snake park and pit, and a crocodile pool.
Nairobi Road, 1.5km from the city centre (tel: 60803/4). Open: daily, 8.30m–6pm. Admission charge.

Ndunga Beach and Fishing Village

This small fishing village is an excellent place to see the traditional lifestyle of the lake fishermen. You can also hire a local fisherman and his canoe for a paddle through the nearby papyrus reed beds to see the hippos and the birds ranging from jacanas to pelicans. Go in the afternoon when the fleet is in.
4km west of the Sunset Hotel. The village is open daily, 8am–6pm. Negotiable fees for photos and accompanied canoe trips.

Kisumu market is one of the largest, most varied and colourful in the country

MFANGANO ISLAND

There are some remote rock paintings and a small fishing community here, but the island has now been taken over as an up-market fishing camp for those wishing to do battle with Nile perch and tiger fish. *55km west of Homa Bay. The only local transport is a twice-weekly ferry from Homa Bay. Visitors to the fishing camp fly in from the Masai Mara. Bookings via Governors Camp, PO Box 48217, Nairobi (tel: 331 871 or fax: 726 427).*

NDERE ISLAND NATIONAL PARK

You can wander freely on foot on this tiny island game park (4.2sq km), which has snakes, hippos, crocodiles, sitatunga and several species of water bird. *Hire a boat from the Kisumu Yacht Club (the round-trip is about six hours, including time for a walk). Alternatively, drive to Kaloka Beach, Seme (40km west of Kisumu) and hire a local canoe. There are no facilities. Admission free.*

RUMA NATIONAL PARK

A 120sq km national park enclosing the Lambwe Valley, Ruma is 10km from the shore of Lake Victoria and boasts Kenya's only herd of roan antelope. *The gate is 32km southwest of Homa Bay (tel: 0385-22007). Open: daily, 6am–6pm. Admission free.*

RUSINGA ISLAND

Mary Leakey found the skull of 3-million-year-old *Proconsul Africanus* here. Today, the island houses an exclusive fishing camp and the mausoleum of Tom Mboya (1930–69), a great nationalist leader, assassinated in Nairobi in 1969. *40km west of Homa Bay, along an appallingly rough road. The island is connected to the mainland by a causeway. Most people fly in from the Masai Mara. Rusinga Island Club (tel: 447 224/8; fax: 447 268).*

Sunset over Lake Victoria from Rusinga Island

THE WESTERN HIGHLANDS

KERICHO

Kericho itself is a small, pleasant, up-country town whose architecture and ambience has changed little in the last 30 years. The real reason for coming here is for the massive Brooke Bond tea plantations, a veritable sea of neatly trimmed green velvet which sprawls out from the town and over the hills for miles around. It seems to go on forever, punctuated only by the women in thick plastic aprons who force their way through the tightly planted bushes, throwing the shoots over their backs into great wicker baskets. It is hard to imagine there are enough people in the world to drink it all.

For a formal tour, make arrangements in advance through the Kenya Tea Development Authority, Rahimtullah Trust Tower, Moi Ave, PO Box 30213, Nairobi (tel: 221 441).

Tea pickers in protective pinafores of Brooke Bond colours

pieces a final polish.

Turn left off the Homa Bay road 11km beyond Kisii. Tabaka village is 6km further on. The quarries, on the far side of the hill, work from Monday to Friday, 8am–5pm. Continue on to Rongo and turn right to get back on to the main road.

Fast growing pine and eucalyptus are popular timber crops in the highlands

TABAKA

This small village is the home of all the pastel pink and white soapstone on sale in Kenya. Everyone in the village is involved in quarrying or carving, and every household has a small array of carvings laid out beside the front door. There have been quarries here since the 1920s, but there is no danger, as yet, of supplies running out. Three quarries are currently being worked, each employing up to 50 people. The carvers (all men) pay about 3,000 shillings for a lorry load of up to 8 tonnes of the stone – a three-month supply. Most can turn out between six and ten carvings a day, dependent on size. The women carry the sackloads of stone from the quarries to the co-operative office and give the

The Coast

A great sweep of palm–fringed silver sands, mangrove swamps and gentle turquoise creeks, Kenya's 480km-long coast gazes calmly out across the coral reefs to the open sea. It is hard to envisage it as a key to the great Indian Ocean trading routes and the centre of the Swahili culture, one of black Africa's most enduring civilisations. It seems too peaceful to have known the many bloody wars that have rocked its shores, as the great maritime powers of the world battled to gain control of its sheltered harbours.

Today, Mombasa is still, quietly, a great trading centre, with a massive, modern port. It has a large Asian population which keeps to itself, and although it is

A perfect day for sailing at Nyali Beach

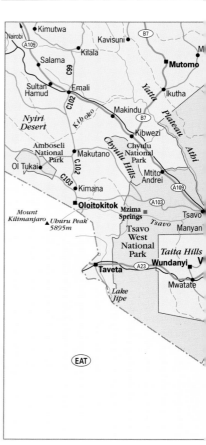

used as a scapegoat by Africans and Europeans alike, it makes money hand over fist. The rest of the population is a motley collection of tribes from all over Kenya. The original Swahili people in the city have long been absorbed into the mainstream, but those in the villages still live a traditional life as small-scale farmers and coastal fishermen. The whole region is strongly Islamic.

Meanwhile, the coast has had a new incarnation as a popular holiday playground. More and more resort hotels line the coast, but most, though large, are still low key. People come here to snorkel on the reefs, for the deep-sea fishing and above all, to sprawl out under a tropical sun and the coconut palms, on a beautiful and still relatively empty beach.

THE COAST

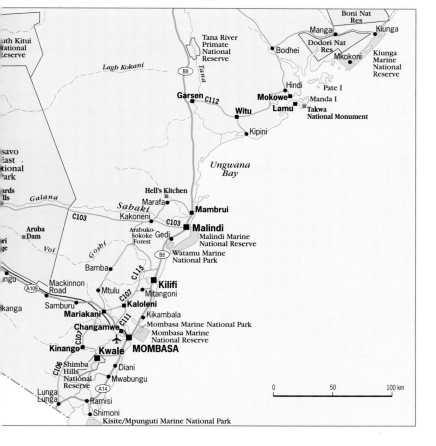

LAMU

Lamu is an enchanted archipelago of low coral islands, sand dunes and mangroves, calm creeks and sailing *dhows*, cut off from the mainland and the rest of the world. Lamu Town, like so many of the towns along this coast, was a great Swahili trading centre, but its island fastness protected it from the ravages of the Portuguese and the Galla tribe, and here alone there is a continuity of history and architecture.

The area became notorious in the 1960s as one of the great hippy hang-outs, but in more recent years the locals reached breaking point and cleared the drugs and nudists from their beaches. In addition, the island's inaccessibility and the efforts of historians have, so far, combined to save the area from mass-market development. Tourism is important here, but it is small scale,

designed for those who are willing to merge unobtrusively with the local lifestyle. There are no discos and little alcohol but the people are friendly, the seafood is wonderful and the atmosphere so laid back it's horizontal.

LAMU TOWN, see **Lamu Town Walk**, pages 118–19.

MANDA ISLAND

Home of the airport, Manda Island is the gateway to Lamu. It also has wonderful beaches, a line of coral reef running along the western shore, a large creek thickly hung with mangroves and the ruins of ancient Takwa.
*Directly across the channel from Lamu Town (see **Lamu Boat Tour**, pages 120–1).*

Lamu Museum is one of many elegant colonial houses on the town's waterfront

MATONDONI

A small village on the west of Lamu Island, Matondoni has long been famous as a *dhow*-building centre. It is possible to wander through the yards, watching the villagers at work building or repairing the boats.

2 hours by foot or dhow *from Lamu Town.*

PATE ISLAND

This remote island has three historic towns – Pate, Siyu and Faza – as well as numerous, largely unexcavated ruins. This was, and is, the other main population centre in the Lamu archipelago, but after centuries of in-fighting Lamu won a decisive victory when it massacred the Pate fleet at Shela in 1812. Since then, Pate has been sliding inexorably into decay.

Probably founded in the 14th century, Pate Town has some old, but poorly maintained Swahili houses. Near by are the overgrown ruins of the original 13th-century **Nabahani** settlement. In the centre of the island, **Siyu** was founded in the 15th century, and between the 17th and 18th centuries became a major centre of Islamic studies. Now much smaller, it still retains a formidable fort dating from the 19th century.

Directly south of Siyu, the ruined city of **Shanga** was built in the 10th century only to be abandoned in the 14th. **Faza**, on the north coast, is now the provincial government headquarters. It is an old settlement, but has been destroyed so many times that the vast majority of its buildings are modern.

19km northeast of Lamu Town. Access by dhow *or local motor launch, then on foot. You will need to spend the night on the island, so be prepared to camp or stay with a local family.*

Boatman punting his *dhow* through the shallow swamps on Manda Island

SHELA

This is the nearest village to Lamu Town and is at the start of a spectacular 11km-long beach. Although an ancient settlement, it has few old buildings other than the 1829 **Juma'a Mosque** and is best known now as the island's up-market resort.

*Shela village is a 45-minute walk from Lamu Town; the beach stretches out beyond that. See also **Lamu Boat Tour**, pages 120–1.*

The excruciatingly uncomfortable bus from Mombasa to the Lamu ferry is not recommended because of poor security on the road. There are regular planes from Mombasa and Malindi. The only public transport on the island is by *dhow* or donkey. Remember that the islands are strongly Islamic. Topless bathing or walking round town in a swimming costume is deeply offensive, and you can only get an alcoholic drink in the resort hotels. There are excellent local guides on sale at the Lamu Town Museum.

MALINDI

One of the greatest and friendliest of the medieval city states along the Kenya coast, the king of Malindi opened up diplomatic relations with China during the voyage of the great explorer Zheng He, in 1414. He sent a present of a giraffe, an oryx and a zebra to the Chinese court and the giraffe was so well received that it became the Chinese symbol of Perfect Virtue, Perfect Government and Perfect Harmony. A later king of Malindi was also the first to offer the hand of friendship to Vasco da Gama, in 1498. When the explorer returned the following year, the first Portuguese trading post was set up here, and the doors of East Africa were opened to Europe.

These days, however, Malindi is a rather tatty resort town, largely owned by Italians. It has numerous hotels, and several restaurants and discos, but daytime activities are clearly focused on the sea. Its beaches are excellent, with none of the seaweed that plagues those further south, and the coral reefs are very accessible – you can even walk to some at low tide. There is brilliant diving and snorkelling although some of the coral itself has been badly damaged by careless flippers. Malindi and Watamu are also Kenya's main centres for deep-sea fishing, made popular, like so many other places, by that obsessively macho sportsman, Ernest Hemingway.

120km north of Mombasa. There is an airport 2km south of the town and a small tourist office on the Lamu road (tel: 21171).

One of the livelier back-streets of Malindi town

THE CROCODILE PARADISE

A small, but attractive park with the usual array of giant tortoises and terrapins, snakes (from cobras and mambas to pythons) and crocodiles. The tour guides are more enthusiastic than knowledgeable and are eager for you to handle some of the livestock, under supervision, including baby crocodiles and terrapins, and a very large python.

About 5km south of the town, near the entrance to the Malindi Marine Park. Open: daily, 9am–5.30pm; feeding at 4pm on Wednesday and Friday. Admission charge.

JUMA'A MOSQUE

The largest of Malindi's 12 mosques, this is a modern building on the site of the old slave market. Among the graves beside it is a 15th-century pillar tomb belonging to Sheikh Abdul Hassan. In the heart of the old town, near the beach.

MALINDI MARINE NATIONAL PARK

This 6sq km national park, together with the surrounding 213sq km reserve and the Watamu Park (see page 101) make up a biosphere reserve that takes in a 30km-long stretch of coast, including the shore, with its mix of mangroves and

casuarina trees, and the coral reef.
Most of the hotels run boat trips to the reef,
but the park entrance and the mass of small
boats for hire are about 6km south of the
town, at the end of the hotel strip. Open:
daily, 7am–7pm. Admission charge.

PORTUGUESE CHURCH

Built in the early 16th century and
surrounded by the old Malindi cemetery,
this tiny, square whitewashed chapel is
thought to have been the first Christian
church in East Africa. In 1542, St
Francis Xavier buried two soldiers here
during his journey to India. Inside is a
faint mural of the Crucifixion.
The southern end of the beach road. At the
time of writing, it was locked up and used as
a storeroom.

VASCO DA GAMA CROSS

In 1499, Vasco da Gama erected a
simple cross of Lisbon stone on a coral

The Town House beach bar

rag base at the entrance to the bay. The
cross itself is original, but the base is a
16th-century replacement, later
concreted in to position.
On a rocky headland at the southern end of
the bay. Access across the bay or via a
footpath off the beach road.

The Vasco da Gama cross, set up to
commemorate the explorer's visit to Malindi

MALINDI ENVIRONS

ARABUKO-SOKOKE FOREST

A 417sq km forest reserve, Arabuko-Sokoke protects one of the last large stretches of dense, ancient coastal forest in Kenya. With numerous rare trees, plants and butterflies, it is also a haven for a variety of endangered creatures such as the grey-white Sokoke scops owl, the Zanzibar sombre greenbul, the 35cm-high Ader's duiker and the yellow-rumped elephant shrew.

The forest stretches south from Gedi to Kilifi. Open to the public with permission from the forestry department. Admission free.

GEDI

This 18-hectare ruined city flourished from the 13th to early 17th centuries.

Gedi ruins, remnants of a great town hidden in the forest

Archaeological finds, ranging from Ming porcelain and Persian glazed ware to a Venetian bead, make it clear that this was a comfortable, if not rich, trading port (the sea has now retreated about 5km).

Gedi was destroyed twice; the first time probably by Mombasa in about 1530, the second by the Galla tribe 200 years later (see pages 106–7). Its name means 'precious' in Galla, but the town was never of great importance and is not mentioned in early travellers' accounts of the coast.

The ruins have long been swallowed up by the forest, with the coral walls set in deep green, dappled glades surrounded by baobab trees hung with lianas. It is a wonderfully atmospheric place at the centre of numerous local superstitions and ghost stories. The excavated section, just inside the northern stretch of the double ring of city walls, must have been the wealthy part of town because it contains the 15th- and 16th-century Great Mosque and Palace. Next to these is a tight web of 14 stone-built houses, such as the House of the Ivory Box and the House of the Chinese Cash, named by romantic archaeologists after the finds found inside them. Also in this area are several pillar tombs, including the Dated Tomb with the Arabic date AH802 (1399) inscribed on it. Near by, the Tomb of the Fluted Pillar marks a pathway to the House of the Dhow (with a *dhow* etched into an inside wall). Many of the living areas have deep wells and sophisticated toilets that are a major source of fascination.

A small site museum contains many of the finds, which range from pottery jars to personal possessions such as an iron lamp, scissors, and a bronze eye pencil. Just outside the historic site is a reconstructed Giriama folk village.

Sunset over the mangrove swamps of Mida Creek, near Watamu

Many of the forest creatures from Arabuko-Sokoke can also be found on the forest trails around Gede. Watch out for giant land snails, giant millepedes and black mambas!

1.5km off the main Mombasa road, 16km south of Malindi. Open: daily, 7am–6pm. Admission charge. There is an excellent guidebook and site plan on sale at the ticket office.

WATAMU

Once a peaceful little fishing village, the great curve of Turtle Bay has now become a small resort town and one of the country's key centres for snorkelling, diving and fishing. The attraction, apart from a beautiful beach and crystal clear, warm water, is the superb coral reef in the 10sq km **Watamu Marine National Park**. This is one of the finest in Kenya, a dazzling playground for fish and sea creatures of every hue, a wonderland where fish come to tap on your goggles and urchins wave as you pass.

Just south of Watamu beach, **Mida Creek** is a large area of tidal mudflats, mangrove swamps and reeds that offer perfect conditions for many wading birds, such as stints, sandpipers and plovers. Between March and May, and August to October, the permanent residents are joined by great flocks of migrants. Many birds that breed in Europe spend the winter here. Near the creek, the underwater **Tewa Caves** are the breeding ground for a colony of gentle-giant rock cod, up to 400kg and 2m long, who will feed from the hands of divers.

About 23km south of Malindi, off the main Mombasa road. Most of the hotels offer trips in glass-bottomed boats, snorkelling and diving. Alternatively, you can hire a boat from the beach or at the entrance to the Marine Park, just south of the Turtle Bay Hotel. Admission charge.

Mombasa

A thousand years ago, when many Western cities were little more than muddy villages, Mombasa was a sophisticated city. By the 15th century, it was trading regularly with Persia, China and India, and its merchants were said to be so rich they wore cloth made of gold.

The end of that century, however, spelt the end of the golden age. In 1498, Vasco da Gama arrived and although he found the town hostile, it was a rich prize and the Portuguese sacked Mombasa four times over the next 90 years. Meanwhile, a new enemy, the ferocious Zimba tribe, was sweeping down the coast, burning and destroying. By 1589, Mombasa was too weak to fight back and the city finally fell to the Portuguese. Plagued by disease and warfare, they

Triumphant tusks curve over Moi Avenue, Mombasa

remained in control until 1697, when a prolonged Omani siege drove them out. There was one last hiccup of Portuguese rule, from 1728 to 1729, but Mombasa soon reverted to the Arabs.

In 1741, the local hereditary governors, the Mazruis, broke away to create an independent state. Battling constantly against the Omanis, in 1824 they called in the British to establish a protectorate but this lasted only until 1826. In 1837, the city fell, the Mazruis were exiled, and the state once again became part of the Omani Sultanate of Zanzibar.

Meanwhile, commercial Mombasa was growing fat again, this time on the profits of the slave trade. As British interest in the region grew, it became the base for the exploration of the hinterland, and in 1888 the Imperial British East Africa Company set up its headquarters here. In 1895, the British leased a stretch of the coast from the Sultan of Zanzibar, and Mombasa came under British rule. It still officially belonged to Zanzibar until ceded to independent Kenya in 1963.

Today, built on a 15sq km island surrounded by a superb natural harbour, the city is still one of Africa's major ports with a population of over half a million. The harbour itself has been transformed into a modern container port and there has been a massive proliferation of tourist resorts on the mainland coasts to the north and south. Mombasa has lost

MOMBASA ISLAND

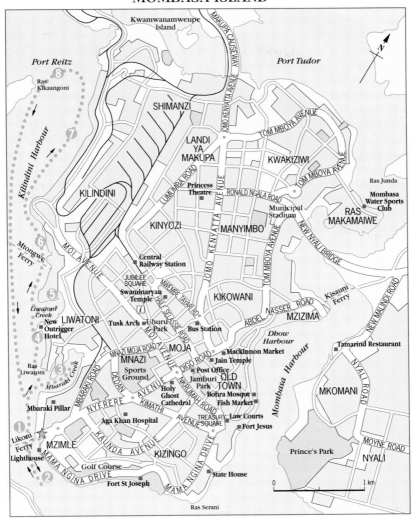

much of its status since the capital moved to Nairobi, however, and although it is noisy and colourful, it is an old-fashioned city whose colonial buildings retain a rather charming air of decaying splendour.

Old Mombasa is still a living community though it has become one of the city's poorer areas

FORT JESUS

In 1593, the Portuguese began work on a fortified stronghold at the entrance of Mombasa Harbour, from which to fend off local hostility and Turkish warships. Designed and built by Italian architect Joao Batista Cairato, Fort Jesus covers about 1 hectare and is roughly rectangular, with bastions at each corner and in the centre of the seawall. The coral walls are about 2.5m wide and 13m high, with a walkway and gun emplacements round the top. The surrounding ditch varies in width from 3m to 12m. There have been many alterations and additions over the years, both by later Portuguese commanders and by the Omanis.

In 1631–2, the fort was occupied during a local Arab revolt. From 1696 to 1698, it was the focus of a great siege by Omani Arabs which eventually broke the Portuguese rule of the coast. In 1895, it

became the local prison. Since 1958, it has been a national monument.

The small museum houses an interesting ceramics collection and the finds from a Portuguese frigate wrecked here in 1697. The 18th-century Omani House, on the Bastion of San António, has displays on Swahili life and fabulous views over the old town. The Captain's Quarters, in the sea wall, were later transformed into a Mazrui Audience Hall. The graffiti includes a eulogy to a Mazrui governor who went to Mecca in 1793.

Next to this, steps lead down to the sea. In the centre of the fort are the remains of several barracks blocks, the old church, a water cistern and a well. *Nkrumah Road, beside the Old Town (tel: 312 839/312 246). Open: daily, 8.30am–6pm. Admission charge. An excellent detailed guidebook is on sale at the ticket office.*

KILINDINI HARBOUR, see
Mombasa Harbour Cruise, pages
124–5.

MAMA NGINA DRIVE

This is a pleasant drive with fine views. A
short distance from the Likoni ferry port,
a grassy picnic area, surrounded by
baobabs, overlooks the harbour entrance
and the south coast. Also on the road are
Mombasa's two casinos, the Mombasa
Golf Club (founded in 1911), the
lighthouse, the Seaport Control Tower
(the coastal radar station) and the
Mombasa State House.
The drive leads around the southeastern edge
of the island from the Likoni ferry port to
Treasury Square (see right).

MODERN CITY CENTRE

The heart of modern Mombasa is tiny, a
cross of four busy roads; Moi Avenue,
Nyerere Road, Nkrumah Road and Digo
Road. The most interesting is Moi
Avenue, which is literally lined by a
double row of souvenir shops and stalls.
It contains the city's most famous
landmark, two pairs of crossed tusks,
created as a triumphal arch to celebrate
the coronation of the British queen,
Elizabeth II, in 1953. Just round the
corner, on Nyerere Road, is the stolid,
neo-Gothic **Holy Ghost Catholic**
Cathedral.

MOMBASA OLD TOWN

Although people have lived here since
the 2nd century AD, virtually nothing
remains of the pre-19th-century city.
Nevertheless, many of the older houses

> '*Mombasa has all the look of a picture*
> *of paradise, painted by a small child.*'
> Karen Blixen, *Out of Africa* (1937)

in the district were modelled on ancient
Swahili designs and reused older doors
and screens. The focus of the city has
shifted and left this as a fascinating
backwater of narrow streets and
crumbling warehouses.
Off Nkrumah Road, near Fort Jesus (see
***Mombasa Old Town Walk,** pages*
122–3).

TREASURY SQUARE

A charming garden square surrounded
by old colonial buildings, this is still the
administrative centre of Mombasa. The
old black and white Treasury Building of
1905 is now the District Administrative
Headquarters, while the cream and white
building next door is the Town Hall. In
the park there is a monument to Allidina
Isram, one of the leading Indian pioneers
of colonial Kenya.
Between Mama Ngina Drive and Nkrumah
Road, near Fort Jesus.

Cannons still line the battlements of Mombasa's
formidable Fort Jesus

SLAVES AND SPICE

Above: Arab traders
march a column of slaves to the coast
Right: Ocean-going *dhows* were the main
trading transport for 1,000 years

In the 7th century AD, Arab and Persian traders brought their *dhows* to the East African coast to trade, and stayed to marry local women. So was born the Swahili people, their name derived from the Arab word *sahel*, which simply means coast. They are not one group, but an array of different tribes drawn together by a common language.

The Arabs brought with them the new religion of Islam, together with education, an urban lifestyle and sophisticated architecture. They built cities of cool, elaborately decorated houses with indoor plumbing and lush garden courtyards.

By the 14th century, they had entered a golden era, trading with Arabia, India and China for glass, porcelain and fine fabrics. Gold, ivory, tortoiseshell and spices were given in exchange, as well as more mundane products such as grain and dried fish. Above all, however, they were slavers, raiding deep into the hinterland, an occupation that has created a profound and lasting mistrust between the coastal and highland peoples.

Nearly destroyed in a series of savage attacks by the Somali Galla tribe in the 17th century, the Swahili had a second flourish of wealth under Omani rule from the 18th to 19th centuries. This only came to an end when they were forced to stop slaving in 1873. Soon after, they came under British rule, and the British wanted control of the trade routes for themselves.

Today, few of the ancient Swahili families survive and while their *dhows* still trade along the coast, they have been largely superseded by modern ships. Still devoutly Muslim, most of the Swahili people now live in small towns and villages, leading more humble lives as farmers and fishermen.

Left: The ruined slaving port of Jumba La Mtwana, whose name means 'House of Slaves'
Below: Mombasa's old slave harbour, now used only by elderly fishing dhows

NORTH OF MOMBASA

KILIFI

This small town has become a popular
centre for watersports and retirement
homes for many white Kenyans. The rich
blue, 15km-long **Kilifi Creek** is a fine
natural harbour and one of the most
beautiful spots along the coast. Recently
adorned by an elegant Japanese bridge, it
often houses smart ocean-going yachts as
well as local fishing boats. Kilifi is also
the major centre of the Giriama tribe, a
Bantu people renowned as sorcerors and
for their dance. The mangrove swamps
inland are home to vast flocks of brilliant
carmine bee-eaters.
54km north of Mombasa.

The mosque at the heart of the Mnarani Ruins

Mnarani Ruins

The ruined Swahili town of Mnarani is
situated in a glorious setting overlooking
Kilifi Creek. Destroyed in the 17th
century by ferocious Galla tribes
rampaging south from Somalia, the town
lay undiscovered for nearly 400 years.
Among the ruins are several pillar tombs
and a mosque with some fine,
fragmentary carvings from the Koran.
*On the south side of Kilifi Creek. Open:
daily, 7am–5.30pm. Admission charge.*

MOMBASA MARINE NATIONAL PARK

An area of 10sq km, surrounded by a
further 200sq km reserve, this is one of
the most accessible of the line of marine
parks that have been set up along the
coast to preserve the fragile coral reef.
There has been some damage to the
coral and the quality here is not quite as
good as in some of the less popular
parks. Nevertheless, it offers some
wonderful opportunities for diving and
snorkelling amid a fantastic array of
multi-coloured fish.
*Just off the Nyali headland, north of
Mombasa, the park can be accessed by boat
at any time (tel: 011-312 744). Admission
charge.*

MTWAPA CREEK

Jumba La Mtwana

One of the chain of Swahili towns which
flourished along the coast until it was
abandoned in the 16th century. No one
is sure why it was destroyed; it could
have been the result of a war between the
Swahili city states or one of the earliest
incursions of the Somali tribes which
eventually spelt the end of Gedi and
Mnarani. It is a fairly small town,
surrounded by baobabs, with the ruins of

MOMBASA ENVIRONS

Map of Mombasa Environs showing locations including:

Ganze, Malindi, **Kilifi**, Kilifi Creek, **Mnarani**, Takaungu, Mitangoni, Kibaoni, Ndzovuni, Dindiri, **Kinuni Ruin**, **Kurwitu Tombs**, B8, Gongoni, Gotani, **Kaloleni**, Kikambala, Mtwapa Creek, **Jamba la Mtwana Tomb**, Shimo La Tewa, Mombasa Marine Nat Park, **Mariakani**, Bamburi Quarry, Nature Trail, Tudor Creek, Freretown, Mombasa Marine Nat Res, Kombeni, Nairobi, Mazeras, **Changamwe**, Mamba Crocodile Village, Nyali, Mwachi, Mkungunjo, **MOMBASA**, Port Reitz, Likoni, (Pemba), Cha Simba, **Tiwi Mosque**, **Kinango**, **Kwale**, Tiwi, **Mwana Mosque**, Diani, Shimba Hills, Shimba Hills National Reserve, C108, Mwabungu, Majimboni, Shimba Hills, Msambweni, **Tumbu Ancient Site**, Ramisi, Kikoneni, Ramisi, Funzi Island, Shimoni, Wasini Marine Nat Park, Wasini Island

Scale: 0 — 10 — 20 km

four mosques, a cemetery and numerous houses. From its name, which means 'House of Slaves', it is clear that this was a major slaving centre as well as trading in goods ranging from ivory to ambergris. There is a small beach set among the mangrove swamps.

16km north of the Mtwapa Creek bridge, signposted off the main Mombasa-Malindi road. Open: daily, 8.30am–6pm. Admission charge.

Kenya Marineland

The largest aquarium and snake park in the area, Kenya Marineland has the normal array of tortoises and turtles, crocodiles and snakes, but also houses the more lethal inhabitants of Kenya's waters, such as sharks and sting rays. The Marineland organises *dhow* trips (see page 155) and African entertainments.

1.5km off the main Mombasa-Malindi road (tel: 485 248). The turn-off is clearly signposted just north of the Mtwapa Creek bridge. Open: daily, 8.30am–6pm. Admission charge.

Shells heaped up for sale on the coast

NYALI

Stretching from Tudor Creek to Mtwapa Creek, just north of Mombasa Island, Nyali was the first area of the coast to be developed for tourism and today has the widest selection of resorts and other attractions in the region.

Bamburi Quarry Nature Trail

In 1971, agronomist Rene Haller began his rehabilitation of this vast, ugly quarry. The result is an unmitigated success story – a delightful, shady complex covering more than 2sq km. It is at once a wildlife sanctuary, an award-winning conservation centre, and a working organic farm that produces everything from fish and crocodiles to coconuts and timber. It has also become one of the main tourist attractions on the coast. Feeding time is at 4pm.
10km north of Mombasa on the main Malindi road (tel: 485 729). Open: daily, 2pm–5pm. Admission charge. See also **Bamburi Quarry Nature Trail** *walk, pages 126–7.*

FRERETOWN

Now dwarfed by a forest of hotel signs, Freretown was established in the 19th century as Kenya's first colony for freed slaves by Sir Bartle Frere, a former British governor in India. Look for the free-standing bell beside the main road, erected by anti-slaving missionaries to ring a warning whenever a slave ship hove into sight.
At the corner of the Nyali turn-off on the main Malindi road, just north of the Nyali Bridge.

Mamba Crocodile Village

This is one of the largest crocodile farms in Africa, with over 10,000 inmates. The pens are set in magnificent botanic gardens, which include a fine orchid collection and an alarming spiders' corner. There is a small aquarium with beautifully designed tanks and both horses and camels are available for rides. Other facilities include a bar, a restaurant and a disco. The crocodile feeding time is at 5pm.
Opposite the Nyali Golf Club on the main Malindi road, about 7km north of Mombasa (tel: 472 709/341/361). Open daily 8.30am–5.30pm. Admission charge.

Water-slides

A fairly modest collection of fun water-slides that are nevertheless the best the coast has to offer and popular with children and local youths alike.
Mombasa Beach Hotel (tel: 471 861), clearly signposted from the Nyali turn-off. Open to non-residents, daily, 8am–6pm. Admission charge.

TAKAUNGU

The oldest slaving port on the Kenya coast, Takaungu is now a charming Swahili village, strung out along a twisting turquoise creek overhung by wooded cliffs, and best known for its ornate wood carving. At the centre of the village is the tomb of the last Mazrui Sultan of Mombasa, who was overthrown and exiled to Takaungu in 1837. Near by, steps lead down to the creek which is used as the local laundry and swimming pool. At the far end of the village, a footpath leads to a small, but delightful beach.
Turn off the Mombasa-Malindi road 10km south of Kilifi and follow the dirt road for a further 5km.

SOUTH OF MOMBASA

The south coast was once remote territory, completely covered by the rich

Somnolent and sun-dried tourists under the palms on Diani beach

primeval **Jadini Forest**, of which only a few tiny fragments now remain. The area was notorious for its slaving activities and later for its huge coconut and sugar plantations, but the development of Diani Beach has brought it into the mainstream of Kenya's tourist industry. In the rarely visited far south there are some of the coast's finest coral reefs and deep-sea fishing grounds. There is a good road all the way down, reached via the Likoni ferry from the south end of Mombasa Island.

DIANI BEACH

Over 10km long and fringed with coconut palms, this stretch of dazzling white sand is a picturebook version of the perfect tropical beach. As a result, it has drawn developers like flies and is now covered by wall to wall resorts. They all have large grounds and, effectively, private beaches. Most of the hotels provide watersports, boat trips out to the coral reef, and some evening entertainment, but there are few other activities on offer and the main problem can be 'cabin fever'.

At the far north of the beach on the Mwachema Estuary, next to the Indian Ocean Beach Lodge, stands the well-preserved 15th-century **Mwana Mosque**. On the southern section, opposite the track leading to the Trade Winds Hotel, stands a giant baobab, 22m in girth and so big it has been protected by presidential decree.

40km south of Mombasa. The access road links to the beach road at the centre of the hotel strip. Consult the forest of signs about which way to turn. It is not safe to walk around at night.

Deep-sea game fishing is one of the most popular – and expensive – entertainments on the coast

MSAMBWENI

An isolated and, until recently, neglected fishing village in lovely surroundings, Msambweni is only visited by those looking to get away from it all. Msambweni ('Place of the Antelope') is another of the many old slaving towns along this coast and still has the remains of a 17th-century slave pen. The energetic can scramble over the coral outcrops along the beach and, at low tide, walk across to **Funzi Island**. This small island recently joined the tourist beat with the addition of a luxury lodge for deep-sea fishermen.

Turn off the main Mombasa road about 50km south of Likoni.

SHIMONI

Another small and run-down town with a significant historic pedigree, Shimoni takes its name (the 'Place of the Hole') from a massive 15km-long cave which was used as a slave pen. It is possible to explore the cave and see the shackles still

bolted into the walls. Take a powerful torch and wear sensible shoes.

In the late 19th century, Shimoni was also the first and short-lived headquarters of the Imperial British East Africa Company, under Sir William Mackinnon. Today, it is increasingly popular as the jumping-off point for some of Kenya's best deep-sea fishing grounds and coral reefs. As yet, however, there is little development.

Coral Gardens

There are now three conservation areas in the coral gardens off the Shimoni coast; the **Wasini Marine National Park**, surrounding Wasini Island and three smaller coral islands just off its coast; the 28sq km **Kisite Marine National Park** and the 11sq km **Mpunguti National Reserve**, which together form one block a little further out to sea.

Fringed with anemones and decorated by star fish, the reefs here are truly spectacular. Great shoals of shimmering psychedelic fish create an enchanting kaleidoscope of ever-changing colour. The coral here is alive and healthy, as yet largely undamaged by anchors and clumsy flippers.

Wasini Island

A small island (only 17sq km), Wasini is a delightful place for walking. Only a pillar tomb set with Chinese porcelain remains of the ancient Arab settlement, but the fishing village is a friendly place where the locals are happy to chat while mending their nets. Try beachcombing – there are plenty of fragments of pottery and glass as well as marine life in the rock pools.

Shimoni is 100km south of Mombasa. Turn off the main road to the Tanzanian border

at Ramisi, and Shimoni is 3km further on.
There are two lodges in Shimoni but only
*camping on Wasini Island. The **Ras***
***Mondini** restaurant runs luxury dhow*
trips to the reef and it is also possible to hire
a small local boat. Some of the deep-sea
fishing and diving operators (see pages
162–3) run boat-based safaris to this area.

TIWI BEACH

The first stretch of the south coast to be
developed, Tiwi has now carved itself out
a niche as the backpackers' paradise, the
only beach near Mombasa to offer a
reasonable selection of self-catering and
low-budget accommodation. This is one
of the widest beaches on the coast, a
plentiful sea of sand and palms with
room to sprawl and walk without too

many other people getting in the way.
Like other beaches in this area, however,
the water itself is full of seaweed. The
Mwachema river estuary divides Tiwi
from Diani Beach and at low tide, it is
possible to wade across to the Mwana
Mosque (see page 111).

Turn off the main Mombasa road about
20km south of Likoni. The beach is 3km
from the turning. Do not walk along this
stretch of road as it is notorious for
muggings.

Right: bulbous mayotte anemone in the Wasini
coral gardens

Below: a clown fish with eggs seeks shelter
under a rock ledge

SOUTHERN GAME PARKS

AMBOSELI NATIONAL PARK

Second in popularity only to the Masai Mara, Amboseli covers 329sq km on the Tanzanian border. Rarely reaching over 1,000m, most of the land is low and flat, and covered by savannah and acacia scrub. The eastern section of the park is dry as a dustbowl with virtually no life except for the odd desert-loving Grant's gazelle. From here, however, the view is unsurpassed, as the animals stand in silhouette against the looming bulk of Mount Kilimanjaro.

In the centre of the park, a rich reedbed surrounds the swamps created by three springs which feed off

underground rivers flowing from Kilimanjaro. As you draw near the water source, the concentration of game intensifies with large herds of plains animals from Thomson's gazelles to zebra. Closer still, happy animals from wildebeest to elephant wallow in the mud, while around them crowd flocks of yellow-billed oxpeckers and cattle egrets, picking the ticks off their backs and snapping at insects churned up by their feet.

Most of the western section of the park is taken up by what used to be a dried up lake bed. Over the last couple of years, this has begun to fill again,

---

KILIMANJARO

Although actually in Tanzania, Mount Kilimanjaro ('the shining mountain') is one of the great sights of southern Kenya. Visible for hundreds of kilometres around, its smooth, rounded, ice-capped summit floats in the sky like a giant, cream-topped Christmas pudding. If you wish to see it clearly, get up at dawn when, for a few short moments, it is free of the ring of clouds that lift it away from any contact with the mundane earth.

At 5,895m, Kilimanjaro is the highest mountain in Africa and also the largest free-standing mountain in the world. In geological terms it is young, a dormant volcano thrown up a million years ago. The fit and determined can climb it with relative ease, although to start an ascent you must go to Arusha in Tanzania; information from the Mountain Club of Kenya (see page 161).

creating a large, shallow soda lake with an increasingly varied bird population ranging from crowned cranes to white pelicans.

240km southeast of Nairobi (tel: 0900/1/2). There are several good lodges and campsites. Access by road and air. Open: daily, 6am–6pm. Daily admission charge.

SHIMBA HILLS NATIONAL RESERVE

This small park covers 192sq km of low-lying hills. Much of it is covered by the dense forest which once stretched over the whole coastal area, and many of its giant trees are thought to be over 1,000

Mount Kilimanjaro, Africa's highest mountain, at 5,895m

years old. There is a high concentration of game here, including Kenya's only herd of the magnificent sable antelope, but the undergrowth is so thick that the animals can be hard to spot. The best way to see them is to stay overnight at the lodge, a tree-hotel built above a waterhole and salt-lick.

30km southwest of Mombasa (tel: 0127-4159/4166), the access road is just north of Diani Beach. Lodge bookings via Block Hotels (see page 171). Open: daily, 6am–6pm. Daily admission charge.

TAITA HILLS

When Tsavo National Park was created, the 1,000m-high Taita Hills were being used for agriculture and the boundary looped round them. The sisal plantations are now defunct and the area has been converted into a private game sanctuary almost enclosed by, and acting as an extension of, Tsavo. Because of the hills, this is a green, well-watered area, in many ways more heavily populated with game than the park itself. The sanctuary's lodges have created their own waterholes and salt-licks and lay bait for nocturnal predators. You can go on night drives and guided walks, and there are balloon flights from the Taita Hills Lodge (see page 139).

Privately owned Taita Hills reserve is tucked in between Tsavo East and West

TSAVO NATIONAL PARK

Originally designated a national park in 1948, covering a massive 20,812sq km (over 4 per cent of Kenya's total area), Tsavo proved too unwieldy to police and has now been split into two, Tsavo East and West. The park varies in height from 200 to 2,000m, but the vast majority is made up of dry, flat plains.

There is a wide range of animals and birds here, but Tsavo has traditionally been famous for its elephants. In the 1950s, before the poachers got to work, there were some 40,000 here, including many huge tuskers – enough for the elephants to strip away all the natural heavy woodland, leaving behind the grass and shrubs that are the main vegetation today. By the time the ivory ban was implemented, there were under 5,000 elephants left. Today numbers are gradually beginning to increase, but most are still immature and it will take decades before the huge tusks are on show again. The elephants love bathing in the pervasive red dust and it is said that by moonlight this is the only place in the world to see real pink elephants.

Tsavo East

Because it is so accessible, Tsavo has always been one of the most popular of Kenya's parks, but there are huge areas completely closed to the public, such as the whole of Tsavo East, north of the Athi and Galana rivers. The southern, accessible section of the park includes the **Kanderi Swamp**, and the man-made **Aruba Dam** on the Voi river, both of which have high concentrations of game. The **Voi Safari Lodge**, near the southern boundary, is set up on a clifftop overlooking a waterhole in what must be one of the most dramatic settings in the country.

Elephant numbers are slowly beginning to recover with the collapse of the ivory trade

Tsavo West

In the northwestern corner of Tsavo West is the **Shetani Lava Flow**, a massive 50sq km lava bed. The name means 'devil' in Swahili and this eerie field of black rock was created some time in the last 500 years by an eruption in the nearby Chyulu Hills, where you can still see the raw cone at the centre of the drama.

Nearby, the **Mzima Springs** form a delightful oasis. Thought for many years to have been created by the eruption in the Chyulu Hills, it is now known that the underground river which feeds the springs is actually part of the Kilimanjaro water system. A massive 282,000 litres per minute pump to the surface, of which a small fraction is diverted into a pipeline to form Mombasa's main water supply. The rest joins the Tsavo river, 7km away. Since 1969, a submerged viewing tank allowed visitors to watch the underwater antics of a hippo colony – until the hippos moved. It is still a pleasant place to dream in the company of the fish.

Tsavo is roughly halfway between Mombasa and Nairobi (220km to each), and the main road and railway line run right through the park. Due to the security situation, a convoy system is currently operating on the road from Amboseli through the western section of Tsavo. Tsavo East, tel: 0147-2211; Tsavo West, tel: 900, ask for 39. Open: daily, 6am–6pm. Daily admission charge.

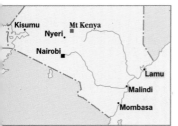

Lamu Town Walk

Lamu dates from 1350, but was built on an earlier 9th-century site. The whole town has been designated a national monument and massive global interest has provided funding for the careful restoration of the old coral-rag houses. This walk takes you through the narrow streets and alleys to Lamu's most fascinating sights. *Allow 30 minutes walking time and 3–4 hours for sightseeing and pottering.*

Start at the main jetty.

THE SEAFRONT

The busy seafront is a 20th-century addition, created by landfill and lined by colonial mansions with wide verandahs. Loaded donkeys struggle to and from the *dhows*, veiled women chat in huddled groups and men in *kikois* lounge around the boats. Everywhere are piles of coral lime and brick, the island's major export since restrictions were placed on logging mangroves.

Walk towards the old jetty.

PETLEY'S INN

This old colonial hotel, founded by Percy Petley, was famous for its *discomfort* in the 1930s, when visitors often had to cook their own food and claimed that the rats of Lamu were big enough to eat the cats – of which there are still many! The hotel is better now, and its upstairs bar is the only place in town to serve alcohol.

LAMU MUSEUM

Directly opposite the old jetty, this is the old British District Commissioner's house with magnificent carved doors, flanked by cannons used by the British

Donkeys are Lamu's only form of haulage

to bombard the Sultan of Witu in 1892. The museum is excellent, offering a detailed history of the town and region, as well as a specialist exhibition on Swahili lifestyles, *dhows* and two *siwas*, huge ceremonial horns of ivory and brass.

DONKEY SANCTUARY

A small sanctuary set up by a British foundation which rescues badly treated donkeys, who are sent out here in order to recuperate and live out their days in warmth and comfort.

Turn left up the narrow alley beside the sanctuary and follow the signs through the web of tiny back streets to the Swahili House Museum.

SWAHILI HOUSE MUSEUM

This fine 18th-century Swahili house was converted into a museum in 1987. The smaller, inner courtyard is surrounded by open rooms ornately decorated with carved plaster niches for the porcelain collection and furnished in traditional Swahili style. Fish were kept in the bath to eat mosquito larvae. Look out for the pasta machine in the upstairs kitchen.

Retrace your steps down through the alleys and turn right on to the main street, one block back from the seafront.

MAIN STREET

Originally Lamu's seafront, this stretch is now the town's main shopping street, a warren of little dark shops and cafés. Go back to browse in the early evening when snacks are roasting over open braziers and the wood-carvers are sitting in their doorways, gossiping as they work.

Walk along the street to the square in front of the fort, at the far end.

LAMU FORT

Built by the Omanis between 1810 and

Coastal fishing *dhow* in the Lamu channel

1821, this massive fort became the town prison from 1910 to 1984. It is now being converted into an aquarium and a maritime and natural history museum. The square around the Lamu fort is home to a busy, colourful morning market.

Turn back towards the seafront and walk along to the starting point.

Lamu Town Museum (tel: 3073) and the Swahili House Museum are both open daily, 8am–6pm (admission charge).

Lamu Fort (tel: 33201; fax: 33402) has recently opened to the public. It is open daily, 7.30am–6pm. Admission charge.

Manda's Mangroves: Lamu Boat Tour

This is a blueprint for the ultimate lazy day, with a little sightseeing, a little sunbathing, and a little sailing. Those in a hurry could cram it into half a day. Take a hat and sunblock as you can get very badly burned on the water.

Hire a dhow *from the main jetty in Lamu town.*

1 THE *DHOWS*

Unlike the giants you see in Mombasa, the *dhows* here are humble wooden sailing boats, similar to those that have been used by the local fishermen for the last 1,000 years. They

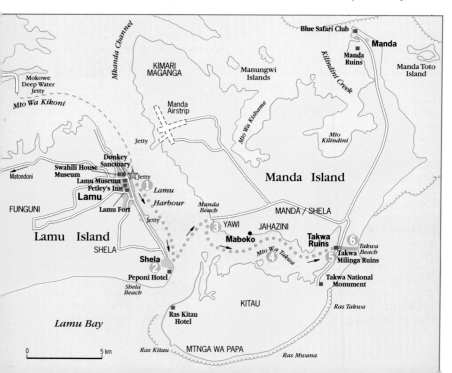

normally have a crew of two; one on the tiller and one to handle the sails.
Sail south along the coast, with excellent views of the Lamu town seafront to Shela.

2 SHELA

Lamu town's nearest neighbour, Shela, is an attractive village with little specific to recommend it other than its superb 11km beach of white-gold sand and dunes. Spend the morning basking in the sun and then head towards **Peponi's**, the best hotel in the vicinity, for a gourmet lunch.

3 FRESH FISH AND AN OPEN FIRE

As an alternative, spend the morning fishing off the *dhow* and land on deserted **Manda Beach**, directly opposite Shela, for a swim and to barbecue your precious catch for lunch. Arrange this with the boatmen the day before and they will provide the extras, such as bread, salad and fruit.

4 THE MANGROVE SWAMPS

From Manda Beach, you sail round into the wide creek which almost splits the island in half. On your left is **Maboko**, a coral mining village which is the only permanent settlement left on Manda. The island was abandoned when the fresh water ran out and the villagers have to import their water from Lamu. As the creek narrows to a watery green tangle of mangrove swamp, the great shiny leaves pressing ever more closely against the side of the boat, it also gets shallower. The boatmen may have to punt through the last narrow channel to Takwa.

5 TAKWA RUINS

The town of Takwa flourished in the 16th and 17th centuries and is thought

Lamu seafront, from the deck of a *dhow*

to have been founded by people fleeing from warfare on the mainland. Strategically situated out of sight of the sea, behind the dunes, it was surrounded by a 2m-high wall. There are 110 known coral-rag houses and stores, all in ruins, but there were also many humbler houses of mud and thatch. In addition, there is a mosque and a fine pillar tomb dated AH1094 (1683). *The Takwa ruins are open daily, 8am–6pm (admission charge). Takwa is only accessible on the rising tide, so the timetable of this tour may have to be rearranged.*

6 TAKWA BEACH

A footpath leads across the dunes to Takwa Beach. Open to the ocean through a gap in the reef, this stretch of shore is subject to large breakers and a strong undertow. **Manda Toto**, to the north, has some of the finest coral in the Lamu archipelago.
Sail gently home as the sunset lights up the Lamu skyline in a blaze of glory and the wail of the muezzin reaches out to tangle with the gusting of the sail.

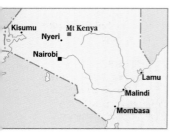

Mombasa Old Town Walk

This is a gentle stroll through the narrow streets of the old town. There are few actual sights, but look for the charming details on the early colonial houses, such as ornately carved doorways and balconies. *Allow 30 minutes plus shopping time.*

Start from Fort Jesus (see page 104). There is an excellent small guide to the Old Town on sale at the Fort.

1 ALI'S CURIO MARKET

Directly opposite Fort Jesus, Ali's Curio Market is one of the friendliest shopping stops in Mombasa. The building was originally constructed in 1898 as the Mombasa Police Station.

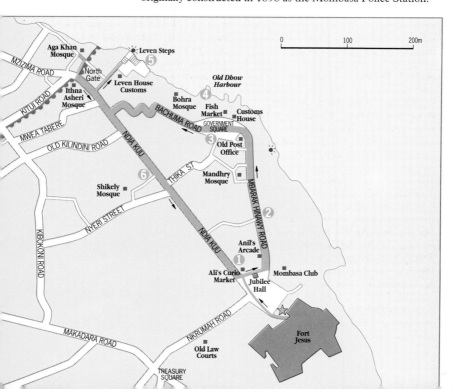

Walk past the shop to the right on to Mbarak Hinawy Road.

2 MBARAK HINAWY ROAD

Once named after Vasco da Gama, this was the route of the hand-pushed trolley buses which were the main public transport system from 1890 to 1923. The road is now named after Sir Mbarak Hinawy, the Sultan of Zanzibar's representative in Mombasa from 1931 to 1959. It has several interesting old houses, such as **Anil's Arcade** (number 3), a three-storey house with tiered balconies. Number 5 and number 9 have some fine Indian plasterwork decoration. Number 10 is the **Mandhry Mosque**, founded in 1570 and the town's oldest mosque still in use. The well opposite is used for ritual ablutions.

Continue on and you come out into Government Square, beside the Old Dhow Harbour.

3 GOVERNMENT SQUARE

This was the real hub of old Mombasa. On your left as you enter, the souvenir shop is the old Post Office, built in 1899 so that Indian railway workers could send money home to their families. At the back of the square is the morning fish market.

4 THE OLD *DHOW* HARBOUR

The old Customs House stands beside the *dhow* harbour. Until Kilindini was founded in 1896, this was the main harbour for East Africa, north of Zanzibar, handling hundreds of trading ships. It is hard to imagine the scene today, when the only boats here are a handful of elderly *dhows*. Small admission charge.

At the far end of Government Square, walk along Bachuma Road and turn right on to

Ndia Kuu. A few metres along, a narrow passage beside a big yellow building of 1906 leads down to the Leven Steps.

5 THE LEVEN STEPS

Named after his ship, HMS *Leven*, these steps were built by a British naval lieutenant, James Emery, who briefly became governor of Mombasa from 1924 to 1926. Today, the steps offer a peaceful viewpoint over the old harbour and across the bay to Nyali.

Return to Ndia Kuu and turn right. The site of the town's old North Gate is quickly reached. A side alley leads to the huge, new shiny Aga Khan Mosque. Turn back and retrace your steps along Ndia Kuu.

6 NDIA KUU

Known by the Portuguese as *La Rapozeira* ('the Foxhole'), the modern name simply means Main Street. There are numerous fine old houses along here with ornately carved doorways, overhanging balconies and even open staircases. Among the finest are numbers 28, 33, and 34.

Ndia Kuu leads straight back to Fort Jesus.

Overhanging wooden balconies

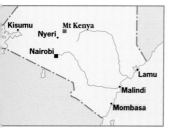

Kilindini Harbour Cruise

Kilindini Harbour was founded in 1896 to handle the increased traffic generated by the East African Railway (see pages 144–5). This boat tour of the vast, bustling, hi-tech harbour offers a very different picture of Kenya. For the route, see the Mombasa town plan on page 103.

The tour leaves from the Likoni Ferry Terminal on the south end of Mombasa Island at 9am, 12pm and 3pm. Tickets are on sale from the Kenya Ferry Authority Office to the right of the ferry port. *Allow 2 hours.*

As you board, take the staircase to the left for the best view. Go mid-week to see the harbour at its busiest.

1 LIKONI

Lively markets have grown up at both ends of the busy ferry, which provides a vital link between the south coast and Mombasa Island. To the right are the huge concrete silos of the Bamburi Portland Cement works.
The boat first turns out towards the open sea.

2 MAMA NGINA DRIVE

Along the clifftop to your left runs Mama Ngina Drive (see page 105). On the headland beyond stand a black and white lighthouse and the Seaport Control Tower, the radar control for all shipping in Kenyan waters.
On reaching the open water, the boat turns back into Kilindini Harbour. Just past the Portland Silos, it turns into the smaller Mbaraki Creek.

3 MBARAKI CREEK

This is the home of the ship repair yards, a hive of activity surrounded by clusters of waiting rust buckets. The huge black tanks on the hill above are used for storing molasses, a major Kenyan export.
Leaving the creek, the boat continues along the line of the island to the right.

4 THE OUTRIGGER

The boat next passes the Yacht Club and, beside the jetty, the New Outrigger Hotel. This is the latest version of the oldest hotel in Kenya, originally built in the 18th century for sailors visiting Mombasa on trading ships. Just beyond

The Likoni ferry is a well-used lifeline for people on the south coast

this, the K-Boats yard hires out boats for deep-sea sport fishing.

5 LIWATONI CREEK

The next turn-off, into Liwatoni Creek, takes you past the Fisheries Department building and the city's main fish market. The large grey building on the clifftop is Bandari College, the Ports Authority training college.

6 MTONGWE

The blue jetty on the right is the terminal of the passenger ferry to Mtongwe. On the south bank (to your left) are the naval and police dockyards, and a large white house, the former home of the Sultan of Zanzibar. Back on the right is the Customs House. Almost constant dredging is needed here to keep the channel clear. Its natural depth is only 13.4m.

7 THE HARBOUR BASIN

Finally you reach the heart of the working harbour with its rows of cranes, and huge ships flying the flags of all nations. The huge red-brick building is the main Ports Authority Office. Ahead, the Kipevu Causeway links Mombasa Island with the mainland. Beside it, vast areas of landfill rubbish tip lie steaming like a science fiction horror story. On your right are the refined oil storage tanks.

8 PORT REITZ

As the boat swings round, you can see the container harbour in the Port Reitz basin, capable of handling as many as 18 super-tankers at any one time. Beside this is the area used for the handling of crude oil.
From here, the boat heads back south to the starting point.

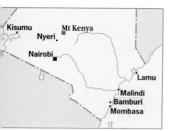

Bamburi Quarry Nature Trail

This gentle stroll through an award-winning reclaimed coral quarry combines game-viewing with a superb, pioneering ecological farm. All walks are guided, so no route has been given (see also page 110). *Allow 2 hours.*

For those arriving on foot from Nyali, or by public transport from Mombasa, 10km to the south, there is a small entrance beside the main road. If you have a car, continue a little further north, through the main entrance of the Portland Cement Factory.

RECEPTION AREA AND TORTOISE LAWN

The reception area and ticket office, the real starting point of the tour, is surrounded by smooth grassy slopes, bordered by small lakes and ponds. The lawns are carefully cropped by giant Aldabra tortoises, some over 100 years old, which are happy to stop munching for long enough to have their necks scratched and photographs taken. There are also a picnic site, a refreshment stand and a lunchtime-only game restaurant here.

GAME SANCTUARY

A short distance on, there is an open fenced area surrounding a small lake. The water is planted with Nile cabbage, an efficient water filter which is harvested as livestock fodder and as a fertiliser. The sanctuary houses many species of wild animal,

including hippos, buffaloes, zebra, waterbuck, oryx, eland and rare Rothschild giraffes. There are also some 160 recorded species of birds.

BAOBAB FARM

Just west of the sanctuary is the working heart of the quarry, Baobab Farm, an ingenious integrated system of ecological farming. The intensive fish farm produces 11 different species of tilapia

Handling a python is an essential part of a snake park tour

Hippos grazing in the ecologically friendly Bamburi game sanctuary

for sale. Any leftovers are fed to the crocodiles in the neighbouring pen. Some of the crocodiles are released back into the wild, others are farmed for their meat and skins. The dirty water from the crocodile pens and the fish farm is used to create and fertilise the rice paddies next door. The paddies filter the water which is then pumped back up to be reused in the fish farm.

FORESTRY AREA

Directly north of the sanctuary, this area was initially planted with trees such as the Australian Casuarina that were able to survive on poor, salty rock. A colony of giant millipedes was introduced to help them create humus. As the soil has improved and the trees have matured, the crop has been harvested for use in construction and as firewood. The area is now being replanted with a variety of over 150 local species, including hardwoods and coconuts. Serval cats and porcupines live in pens under the trees, while vervet, sykes and mona monkeys play in the branches above.

THE NURSERIES

North of the forest area, near the road gate, are an area of mangrove swamp and another working section of the farm that includes the fish and crocodile breeding pens, the fisheries research centre and the plant nursery.

THE SNAKE PARK

Back beside the reception area, a separate entrance leads into the small, walled snake farm, with a wide variety of species, many of which have been collected within the quarry itself. The authorities say they prefer to have their snakes safely away from visitors' feet!

The North

*D*raw a rough line across the map of Kenya from Kitale in the west to the Tana river delta in the east, via Lake Baringo and Isiolo, and everything above it (over two-thirds of the country's area) is termed the North. It is remote, isolated and forbidding. The roads have grandiose names like the Trans-East African Highway or the Great North Road, but in truth, they are often little more than dirt tracks – main roads because they are the only roads.

There are some small patches of lush green mountain, but much of the area is desert scrub where only the hardiest trees and bushes cling to a precarious life, their long tap roots sucking up moisture from deep underground reservoirs. There are many river beds, but they are all dry, only coming to life during infrequent flash floods when brief heavy rains cannot penetrate the rock-hard earth. The contrast from the bright and fertile green of the Central Highlands could not be greater.

The barren shores of Lake Turkana, the most northerly of the Rift Valley lakes

Tiny handfuls of humans roam over hundreds of square kilometres in search of fodder for their herds. At the time of writing, after many years of drought, the herds are almost all dead, their skeletons strewn across the ground, while the few remaining people live beside the road, begging for water from passing motorists as they slowly head into the villages that have sprung up around the food aid stations. Even when the rains come back, it will take years for the area to regenerate.

The only stop on the main tourist circuit is the Samburu National Reserve, just north of Isiolo. A few more

NORTHERN KENYA

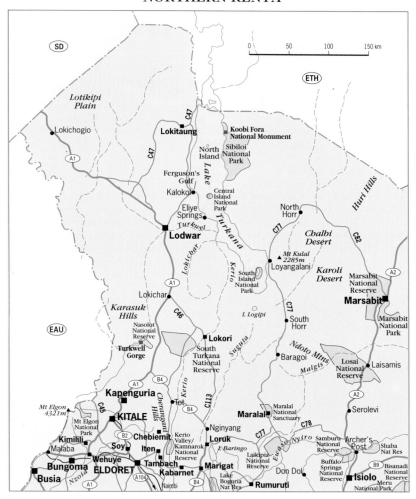

adventurous people will fly, or make the long drive up to Lake Turkana and a mere handful now fly in to Marsabit National Park. There is nothing to attract the visitor in the vast northeastern province, and to add to the normal, very real dangers of desert travel, much of this area has effectively been declared out of bounds by the armed incursions of Somali bandits.

MARALAL

'We arrived in the colourful town of Maralal to discover it wasn't' is how one disgruntled tourist put it. There is a tendency to hype up the town, mainly because it is the last outpost of any sort of civilisation on the long haul up to Turkana. In fact, it is a pleasant little place set in attractive hills that offer some excellent bush walking. In town, there is a small, lively market, and the lodge has a private game park with a large herd of eland. It has some claims to fame; on the hill above the Maralal is the house in which Jomo Kenyatta spent seven years under house arrest, and the famous explorer, Wilfred Thesiger, lived in the town until very recently. Most of all, it

The giraffe-necked gerenuk is found solely in the semi-desert of Northern Kenya

acts as a base for camel trekking, walking and white-water safaris on the Ewaso Nyiro river, about two hours' drive away (see pages 142–3).

Even if you are not going to Turkana, head north for about 30km to **Moridjo**, where there are two utterly spectacular viewing points as the mountains plunge in an almost sheer drop of some 2,000m into the **Suguta Valley**, one of the hottest and most inhospitable regions of the planet. In late afternoon, the light is like a Hollywood set for Armageddon. *356km north of Nairobi via Naivasha and Nyaharuru.*

NORTHERN GAME PARKS

By far the most important game park in the north is the **Samburu National Reserve** (see page 132). There are, however, many others which have not been given full descriptions. Most are difficult to get to, have few facilities and, most importantly, the recent activities of bandits have left tourists vulnerable to attack.

On the edge of the desert outback, due east of Meru (see page 72), is a huge cluster of interlinked parks, around the upper reaches of the Tana river. They are **Meru National Park**, and the **Bisanadi**, **Kora**, **North Kitui** and **Rahole** national reserves. Together they cover 5,281 sq km and encompass almost every form of habitat, from Meru's open woodlands to the dense bush of North Kitui and the dry scrub of Bisanadi. Meru is the most famous, the most accessible, and the only one with visitor facilities. This is where the Adamsons did much of their research and where Joy Adamson was murdered. George Adamson later moved his base to Kora, where he too was murdered. In 1983 to 1984, the English Royal

Grevy's zebras, with their large ears and pop-art stripes, are found only in the north

Geographical Society and the National Museums of Kenya mounted a massive expedition to Kora, one of the world's first and largest studies of an entire eco-system.

Directly north of Samburu are the impenetrable, volcanic **Losai National Reserve** and the **Marsabit National Reserve**. Marsabit is a densely forested mountain park containing two beautiful crater lakes. It was traditionally famous for its giant tuskers, among them President Kenyatta's favourite elephant, Ahmed (see page 47). Poachers slaughtered many of them, but it is still an elephant stronghold, as well as having large herds of greater kudu and many predatory birds, including lammergeiers. It is possible to fly into the park and there is a lodge as well as camping facilities.

Finally come the tiny **Nasolot** and the **South Turkana** national reserves of completely undeveloped scrubby desert to the north of the Marich Pass on the Kitale-Lodwar road.

THE CAMEL DERBY

At the end of September each year, the Yare Safaris Hostel (4km west of Maralal) plays host to the **Maralal International Camel Derby**. An increasingly popular day of sheer mayhem, races are open to all who care to rent a camel, from rank amateurs to international racing jockeys.

In 1993, the first truly gruelling endurance race with huge prizes was run across the deserts of northern Kenya in the month leading up to Derby Day. This has become an annual event.

SAMBURU AND ENVIRONS

Beyond the prairie-like highlands to the north of Mount Kenya, the road falls dramatically by over 1,000m to the hot, dusty lava plains that mark the start of the northern deserts. Here, three easily accessible national reserves on the banks of the Ewaso Nyiro river have become popular stops on the tourist trail. Of the three, the most famous is **Samburu** (239sq km), but it shares a boundary along the river with **Buffalo Springs** (131sq km) and the two act, in effect, as one park. Nearby **Shaba** (239sq km) is far less visited.

At an altitude of between 700 and 1,500m, the landscape is dry and stony, punctuated by small rocky hills, while the vegetation is made up of myriad forms of thorny acacia from small bushes to great yellow-trunked fever trees. The main reason for visiting these parks is to see reticulated giraffe, Grevy's zebra and gerenuk (see **Fauna**, pages 24–31). However, there are also large herds of Beisa oryx and Grant's gazelle, plenty of elephant and, for the really lucky, the rocky hills provide the perfect habitat for leopards. As ever, the skies are full, with over 300 species of bird having been recorded in the park, including several species of eagle and bustard.

About 30km north of Isiolo. Buffalo Springs and Samburu lead directly off the main road to the left, Shaba is a few kilometres off the main road to the right. Report in to the police post at Isiolo before continuing north. All three have lodges and campsites. Open: daily, 6am–6pm. Admission charge.

Samburu Lodge, a haven of comfort on the Ewaso Nyiro river

El Molo fishermen returning home

TURKANA

Inviting and faithless, Lake Turkana shines like jade in the sun, full of promise but barren. Black volcanic lava stretches, unbroken by a blade of grass, to bare, brown hills until the sight of a living tree is cause for excitement. It is compellingly beautiful and cruel.

The greatest and most northerly of Kenya's Rift Valley lakes, Turkana is 257km long, averages 31km in width and covers an area of 7,500sq km, of which 6,400sq km are in Kenya. Fed from the north by the Omo river, which sweeps down off the Ethiopian Highlands, it was, until 2 million years ago, a freshwater lake. Today, Turkana has no outlet and the basin is gradually silting up. It is not a true soda lake, but its alkaline water is only just drinkable.

The first European explorers, Count Samuel Teleki von Szek and Lieutenant Ludwig von Höhnel, arrived in 1888 and named it after Crown Prince Rudolf of Austria. At first sight, they described it as 'a pearl of great price'. Next day they realised that it would not support life and their own lives were at stake. Höhnel wrote: '… like some threatening spectre rose up before our minds the full significance of the utterly barren, dreary nature of the lake district. Into what a desert had we been betrayed!'

Astonishingly, a few people (Turkana, Rendille, Gabra, and El Molo) have adjusted to the bitter heat and desert winds, and manage to scratch a meagre living from the rocks. As the drought intensifies their already desperate plight, they seem even more disposed to fight for territory from which most would thankfully flee.

The easiest way to get to Lake Turkana is by air, but for the adventurous, overland safaris add to the mind-blasting impact of the terrain (see page 143).

THE CRADLE OF MANKIND

Since the 1920s, the story of prehistory in East Africa has been the story of the Leakey family. Louis and Mary Leakey spent a lifetime excavating and studying prehistoric sites along the Rift Valley. At the famous Olduvai Gorge in northern Tanzania, they bumped the date of mankind's origin back about 1.8 million years. In 1967, their son Richard discovered the Koobi Fora fossil site on Lake Turkana (see page 136). Here he not only found an almost intact skeleton of a *Homo erectus* boy,

Left: archaeological evidence suggests that the Great Rift Valley was the birthplace of humanity. Above: stone tools found at several valley sites

about 1.6 million years old, but through other finds, extended the history of mankind back another million years to about 2.9 million BC.

The Rift Valley offers perfect conditions for the study of human prehistory. The relatively recent volcanic activity covered and preserved many remains, much in the same way as the eruption of Vesuvius stopped Pompeii in its tracks. The upward heave of the valley walls has laid these strata open to erosion by wind and rain. In some cases, the fossils literally lie on the surface, waiting for archaeologists to recognise them.

The picture emerging today is very different from the straight linear path of evolution that was believed for so long. During the Pliocene era (1–3 million years ago), the first recognisable modern African mammals were evolving. At the same time, it now seems, three different species of proto-humans – *Australopithecis robustus*, *Gracel man* and *Homo habilis* – lived side by side for over a million years. However, this is a field in which whole theories can rest on a single bone, and the picture is still far from clear. What is evident is that the East African Rift has provided a wealth of specimens, many far older than those found elsewhere, and has an increasingly solid claim to being the birthplace of humanity.

LOYANGALANI

An obscure little settlement, ironically made more interesting by the drought as the normally nomadic Turkana have moved into town. This whole area is part of the 7,000sq km **Mount Kulal Biosphere Reserve**, set up by UNESCO for the study of arid lands. Rising up behind the town to 2,285m, Mount Kulal itself is an oasis of misty montane forest amid the lava flows and craters. It can be climbed by the fit and well-equipped.

North of Loyangalani, the El Molo tribe (the smallest in Kenya with under 500 members) fish and hunt crocodiles for food. Their island homes are flimsy, basket-like affairs in which the children

El Molo boys playing the ancient game of endokive

Life is harsh for the El Molo, bringing their children up in utterly desolate surroundings

and goats live side by side. Off the shore, the 39sq km **South Island** is the tip of a volcano, completely covered in volcanic ash and home only to the odd wild goat. *On the eastern shore of Lake Turkana, a very long 240km north of Maralal. There are two campsites and one lodge. The El Molo village, 6km north of the town, can be reached by a causeway or canoe. The admission charge includes all photographs. Hire a boat in town for the 13km round trip to South Island, but beware of sudden storms.*

SIBILOI NATIONAL PARK

An area of 1,570sq km around the **Koobi Fora** fossil beds (see pages 134–5) has been designated a national park to preserve finds for future archaeologists. Discovered accidentally by Dr Richard Leakey in 1967, this desolate spot has become one of the most important areas for prehistoric research in the world.
120km north of Loyangalani. If you are dedicated enough to try and get there, hire a plane or a boat from Ferguson's Gulf, on the western shore of Lake Turkana (access via Kitale and Lodwar).

GETTING AWAY FROM IT ALL

'The descent of the African night is never forgotten. There is nothing more complete than to rest by a fire on a canvas seat, with tobacco and a drink, as the sky grows blue dark and the stars sharpen with the clarity peculiar to Africa, until the rim of the firelight seems surrounded by a second, outer world alive with the night sounds of contesting animals...'

BARTLE BULL,
Safari (1988)

An elephant pauses to admire its strength in dismembering a tree

GETTING AWAY

The whole point of a holiday in Kenya is to get away from it all. Many of the listings in the **What to See** section take you many miles out into the bush. Getting away from it all here really means getting away from other tourists,

Wildebeest during their annual migration

leaving behind the trappings of sophistication.

The vast majority of the tourists on the coast stay within the stretch from Malindi to Diani Beach. Head north to Lamu or south to Funzi and Shimoni, and you are away from the crowd. Inland, there is a well-worn tourist path to the Masai Mara, Samburu, the Rift Valley lakes, Amboseli and Tsavo. In any of the other game parks, you will leave the herd behind. Even within these most popular parks, it is easy to shrug off the flock of minibuses if you venture into the remoter sections, away from the lodges and airstrips. There are virtually no tourists at all in Western Kenya beyond the Mara, so head over to Lake Victoria or up to Mount Elgon. North of Baringo, the number of other tourists dwindles to a mere trickle, while beyond Maralal, on the road to Lake Turkana, you will feel as if you have stepped off the end of the known world.

BALLOONING

It is so expensive that many people regard a balloon trip as a once in a lifetime treat. The chief problem with this is that once in the air, you never want to come down, and once reluctantly back on the ground, all you can dream of is how to afford another ride.

Up in pitch darkness, blinking and shivering, you arrive at the launch site just as the balloon puffs out, its gaudy orange envelope and the streak of orange flame the only spot of brilliance in the monochrome of early dawn. As you are instructed on how to brace yourself for landing and take-off, it billows high above the trees – so much larger than expected. You climb in, the rim of the basket is reassuringly high, and turn to look at the great jets of flame, while the ground floats gently away from you. You are drifting high above the trees, but there is no sensation of movement, and no sense of panic at being in a basket several hundred metres above the earth.

The sun turns sky and grass alike to gold; below, a herd of nervous wildebeest skitter away from the balloon's shadow. The sharp-eyed pilot points out a cheetah slinking through the grass, a trail of dust across the plains marks the progress of the chase vehicles.

The game-viewing is good, but it becomes almost irrelevant in the whole glorious experience. As the pilot starts, all too soon, to search for a suitable landing place, away from water and free of lions, you will him to go on forever. Your heart crashes back to earth with a bump bigger than that of the basket. All that saves you from dejection is the champagne breakfast laid out behind the rise, a gourmet picnic fit for a king. *Balloon trips operate in the Masai Mara and Taita Hills, near Tsavo. Most safari*

*companies include them as an optional extra. Alternatively, contact **Balloon Safaris** (Nairobi, tel: 502 850 or fax: 501 424); **Adventures Aloft** (Siana Springs, tel: 220 592; fax: 332 170); **Transworld** (Masai Mara, tel: 229 579; fax: 333 488).*

Balloons at dawn are one of Kenya's most romantic experiences

MESSING ABOUT IN BOATS

One of the best ways of getting away is to take to the water, whether on a raft over Class V rapids with your heart in your mouth, on a sea-going yacht with the prospect of wrestling marlin, or a leisurely meander through the mangrove swamps on a *dhow* under sail.

THE AFRICAN QUEEN

Tucked in between the mangrove laden canals of the Tana river delta and the great, gleaming sand-dunes of the Indian Ocean, north of Malindi, stands a small,

Tourist *dhows* offer a variety of entertainment from dinner-dances to acrobats

isolated tented camp. It offers up to 200 species of bird, magnificent game-viewing, utterly private beaches and even a large natural mud-bath, said to be beneficial to the skin. Guided game-viewing is on foot or through the swamps on a motor launch, *The African Queen*, remodelled since it was sunk by Humphrey Bogart.
***Tana Delta Ltd**, PO Box 24988, Nairobi (tel: 882 826 or fax: 882 939).*

DEEP SEA FISHING, see pages 162–3.

DHOWS

There are few sights more elegant than a *dhow* in full sail, and nothing more peaceful than sitting on board, trailing a hand through the spray as the wind catches the great triangular sail and the bow slices through a gentle sea. There are some very up-market *dhow* trips in Mombasa (see page 155) which are a totally different and very worthwhile experience. For the truly off-beat adventure, however, head north to Lamu and take a day trip to nearby islands or venture further afield and sleep under the stars (see pages 96–7 and 120–1). True addicts, with time to spare, can hire a *dhow* for a longer, coast-hugging journey down to Mombasa or even as far as Zanzibar. Sail by day, camp at night around a bonfire, and live on what you can catch over the side.

LAKE VICTORIA

Gone, sadly, are the days when the lake steamer linked Kenya and Tanzania with Uganda. Now the elderly ferry does a slow shuffle along the lake shore between Kisumu, Kendu Bay and Homa Bay. There are three classes, but do remember that this is local transport, rarely touched

For those who can't swim, glass-bottomed boats offer a glimpse of the reef world

by tourists, so don't expect too much, even of first class. You should be able to buy sodas and sandwiches on board, but take your own supplies just in case.

The journey takes five hours each way, and you will have to arrange for return transport, unless you wish to trust to the local bus or *matatus*.

Other local ferries, resembling overgrown canoes, travel between the inhabited islands, and you can hire a boat from the local fishermen to take you out to one of the island game parks or just for a ride.

Tickets for the ferry are available from the jetty offices, just behind the Railway Station in Kisumu, and next to the hotel in Homa Bay.

MOMBASA HARBOUR CRUISE,
see pages 124–5.

WHITE-WATER RAFTING
Kenya has three rivers suitable for rafting – the Tana, the Athi and the Ewaso Nyiro. Most levels of competence can be found, from gentle eddying backwaters to Class V white water to equal the toughest in the world. **Savage Wilderness Safaris** organise tailor-made rafting trips, from gentle one-day excursions to two-week surfeits, though most people find three to four days plenty. You can decide the level of comfort you require (and are willing to pay for), from a bivouac and bonfire to the full works with showers, four-course meals and wine. *Savage Wilderness Safaris, PO Box 44827, Nairobi (tel: 521 590 or fax: 501 754);* **UK** *– 22 Wilson Ave, Henley, Oxon RG9 1ET (tel: (01491) 574 752);* **USA** *– 925 31st Ave, Seattle, WA 98122 (tel: 206/323 1220).*

Samburu man leads a camel during a trek in the Ewaso Nyiro area

SAFARI ADVENTURE

The vast majority of people taking safaris travel with one of a handful of major operators who offer comfort and convenience, travelling in minibuses and staying at lodges and luxury permanent tented camps. The vast majority of safari operators, however, are tiny outfits prepared to take people anywhere and do anything they choose. Some come at a price; others, offering basic conditions, charge rock bottom rates. They all provide a way for the more adventurous to experience the real joys and frustrations of off-beat Africa.

MAKING YOUR SELECTION

You will need to do your homework and a lot of phoning around to find the right selection for your own tastes and pocket. Most importantly of all, think carefully and honestly about what you really want. If you over-estimate your tolerance levels or are too ambitious in your aims, you

will be miserable. Is comfort important, do you want the excitement of roughing it, or would you prefer the half-way stage of camping with a shower and cold beer? Do you want to be off on your own or do you prefer company? Can you put up with the many hours of bumpy travelling over dusty roads required by cheaper safaris or more distant destinations? Will you be driven insane by endless punctures, or are you happy to push when stuck in the mud? Do you want to give up altogether on road transport and take to the bush on foot or by camel? Most important, what can you afford?

CAMEL SAFARIS

You can ride the camel or you can walk while the camel carries the gear. Both are hard work, involving long hours walking or sitting perched on the camel, every nodule of its spine carving you in half, while you think longingly about walking. The camel drivers will assure you that you will be fine after a week – small comfort when the safari is four days long! There is a great thrill about travelling by camel, however, which goes a long way towards making up for the discomfort. You can get far closer to wild animals than in a vehicle and you have a real chance to learn something of the culture of your camel drivers (normally Samburu tribesmen).

SPECIALIST SAFARI OPERATORS

Bike Treks
Walking, climbing and cycling (mountain bike) safaris for the active traveller.
PO Box 14237, Nairobi (tel: 446 371 or fax: 442 439).

Bushbuck Adventures
Off-the-beaten-track walking safaris in relative comfort.
PO Box 67449, Nairobi (tel: 212 975 or fax: 218 735).

Camel Treks Ltd
A major camel safari firm offering three- or five-night safaris weekly during the dry season (closed for the rains from April to June and also between mid-October and November). Contact Let's Go Travel Ltd for details (see page 189).

Cheli and Peacock
Small up-market company combining Landrover and walking safaris with private tented camps.
PO Box 39806, Nairobi (tel: Karuri (0154) 22551 or fax: 22553).

Gametrackers
Rugged, but reliable budget safaris.
PO Box 62042, Moi Avenue, Nairobi (tel: 222 703 or fax: 330 903).

Safari Camp Services
A wide selection of camping safaris at several budgets and levels of comfort.
Koinange Street (PO Box 44801), Nairobi (tel: 228 936; fax: 212 160).

Tony Mills Safaris
Expensive exclusive safaris, custom-built to your requirements. Tony Mills is a great bird specialist.
PO Box 122, Kitale (fax: 0325-2065 or through Karen Connections (tel: 884 091/2 or fax: 882 723).

Sleeping under the stars gives a superb opportunity to see wildlife at night

THE LUNATIC LINE

'What it will cost no words can express;
What is its object no brain can suppose;
Where it will start from
no one can guess;
Where it is going to nobody knows.
What is the use of it none can
conjecture;
What it will carry there's none
can define;
And in spite of George Curzon's
superior lecture
It clearly is naught but a lunatic line.'

and 33,000 Indians were imported as construction workers.

The line ran through swamp, forest, and desert, crossed the Rift Valley and climbed to over 2,743m. There were horrendous problems with theft by local tribespeople, who took the copper wire for jewellery, and the rails for weapons. Disease stalked the camps and 28 men fell prey to

When the Imperial British East Africa Company decided to build a railway line inland from their fledgling colony at Mombasa, no one knew quite what was at the other end. Only a handful of Europeans had ever explored the area, and there was absolutely no development to create a market for either freight or passenger traffic. At a projected cost of £3.5 million, it was one of the most unlikely gambles in colonial history. Henry Labouchère's satiric poem was only one of a frenzy of objections.

Construction on the 935km, metre-gauge track began in 1896. From the start, it proved eventful. All building materials travelled to Kenya via Bombay; a new harbour was built at Kilindini to handle the volume of cargo;

man-eating lions before the culprits were eventually shot, stuffed and put on display in a Chicago museum.

In 1899, Nairobi was founded as a railhead. By the time the line reached Kisumu on the shores of Lake Victoria, in 1901, settlers had followed it inland to what proved to be some of the world's most fertile farmlands. The railway to nowhere had created a colony.

Nairobi station; the land was damp and mosquito ridden when the railhead arrived in 1899

TRACKS ACROSS AFRICA

Winston Churchill, who got to sit on a garden seat on the cowcatcher in 1908, described the East African Railway as the most romantic in the world. Its route from Mombasa, inland across the great Tsavo plains, through Nairobi and the Central Highlands, across the Rift Valley and the great tea plantations, to Lake Victoria is staggeringly beautiful. All the regular trains are overnight, however, giving you tantalising glimpses of what you have missed.

Nevertheless, the train is wonderful – old-fashioned and thoroughly atmospheric. First class has two-berth cabins and second has four. Both have fans, private washbasins, and plentiful, hygienic toilets. Third class offers uncomfortable seats only. For first and second class, you must book ahead and specify whether you want bedding, dinner and/or breakfast. Meals are worthwhile, not for the quality of the food, which is flavourless and institutional, but for the ambience. Served on spotless linen, using china and cutlery left over from the colonial period, the four-course dinner menu, which involves thick, brown soups and stodgy puddings, seems not to have changed since Mrs Beeton was alive and kicking.

At present there is one service nightly between Nairobi and Mombasa, leaving at 7pm. It is relatively smooth journey which offers some chance of getting to sleep. There is also one train each night between Nairobi and Kisumu. There is meant to be a day train between Nairobi and Mombasa at weekends, but it is an on-off affair, so check whether it is running.

Bookings via any Kenyan travel agent, many safari companies, or from station booking offices. Nairobi Station, Station Road, is 1.5km from the city centre; Mombasa Station, Haile Selassie Avenue, is a few hundred metres from Moi Avenue; Kisumu Station, New Station Road, stands between the lakeshore and town centre.

All aboard the Lunatic Line for the 935km journey from Mombasa to Kisumu, Lake Victoria

DIRECTORY

'So geographers in Afric-maps
With savage pictures fill their gaps;
And o'er unhabitable downs
Place elephants for want of towns'

JONATHAN SWIFT,
On Poetry (1733)

Shopping

*K*enya has almost more souvenir sellers per capita than any other country in the world. There are up-market shops, street stalls, market stands, wayside curio shops, wandering touts and tribal women with a few trinkets. Every tour guide has deals going with certain shops; every time you walk down the street, or even stop for a drink, a group will miraculously gather. They are all superb salesmen, pitch an amazing hard-luck story (sadly, often all too true), and haggle until you are ready to drop. What is more, they travel in packs, and as soon as you have made a deal with one, the next steps in. It is often extremely difficult not to buy, and by the time you have 25 unwanted copper bracelets, 10 soapstone rhinos, and an alarmingly vicious Masai spear, you could seriously be questioning your sanity.

The initial price is usually set according to what they think you are willing to spend. Prices start higher on the coast, while an American accent is a real drawback. Luckily, if you bargain hard enough, prices for the often rather poor quality souvenirs at street level can be extremely low. You go away pleased with your haggling skills, while the vendor beams with delight at getting roughly double what it was actually worth.

Prices for real quality are markedly higher, it is best to stick to the up-market, fixed price shops. If the price is not displayed, ask for a receipt to avoid opportunistic money-making by the staff.

A wide range of basketry is available

WHAT TO BUY

BASKETRY

There are many possibilities, from laundry baskets to brightly coloured trays and placemats. Look out in particular for the sisal *kiondos*, which make excellent handbags. The baskets are used by the Kenyans themselves, so tend to be of excellent quality and very hard wearing.

FABRICS

Unless you want to go all out and buy yourself a safari outfit, complete with solar topee, have a good look at the brilliant range of T-shirts. Alternatively, you can buy a *kanga*, the sarong-style cloths worn by local women, with bright designs and often acerbic Swahili proverbs printed on to the hem, or *kikois*, lengths of thicker, often stripy cloth, traditionally worn by coastal fishermen. There is also a wide range of batiks and wax paintings, many of them are of extremely good quality.

MAKONDE STATUES

Usually depicting people, these glossy wood carvings are an imported tradition from Tanzania. Theoretically made of ebony, most are fakes using lighter woods and boot polish. You can feel the difference by weight (ebony is extremely dense and heavy). It is illegal to carve Kenyan (but not imported) ebony, and ecologically unsound to support the trade. Many sculptures are very crudely carved, so shop around.

STONE
Ubiquitous pink and white Kisii soapstone, from Western Kenya (see page 93), comes in every feasible incarnation from hippos to ashtrays and chess sets. There are also many beautiful malachite products, from chess sets to bowls, beads and bracelets, at very affordable prices.

TRIBAL BEADS
Alongside the array of traditional gourds and calabashes, and purely touristy spears and shields, is an array of wonderfully bright and intricate beadwork, from earrings to spectacular Masai wedding necklaces. Easily carried, these make excellent souvenirs, but the workmanship is sometimes shoddy, and because of the amount of detail, they can be surprisingly expensive.

WOOD CARVINGS
Perfect cheap-and-cheerful souvenirs

Masai stools with painted wildlife

which come in every shape and form, from multitudinous small animals to napkin rings and salad servers, and simple, elegant hardwood bowls.

Wood carvings are an excellent buy

> **WARNING**
> There is a worldwide ban on all elephant products, including ivory. Please support this campaign and ignore the few touts still working illegally. You face heavy penalties if caught in possession. The elephant hair bracelets are often fakes, made of grass and boot polish.

WHERE TO SHOP

Shopping hours are normally from Monday to Saturday, 8.30am to 5.30pm. Some shops close for lunch between 1pm and 2pm.

NAIROBI

Nairobi's tiny city centre is crammed with souvenir shops – some undisguised, many masquerading as art galleries. For good quality, try the malls in the New Stanley and Hilton hotels, and Standard Street. For cheaper, reasonable quality goods, the best place is City Market, on Muindi Mbingu Street. For real bargains, try the street stalls along Tom Mboya Street and River Road (not safe on your own), or Kariokor Market, on Racecourse Road. The latter is far closer to being a real market, with thriving local trade as well. The best fabrics and clothes are found in Muindi Mbingu and Biashara streets.

Souvenir stalls line most of Mombasa's main streets

African Heritage Centre

The place to shop in Nairobi, with the best of Kenyan and other African craftsmanship on offer. The newer out-of-town superstore has even more to offer, with minibuses shuttling out from Kenyatta Avenue four times a day. Libra House stays open until 10pm on weekdays for a last shopping spree on your way to the airport.
Kenyatta Avenue (tel: 333 157) and Libra House, Mombasa Road, 7km from the city centre (tel: 554 547).

Kazuri

This bead and pottery factory employs some 150 women. A visit includes a tour of the workshops as well as a superb range of beads on sale in the factory shop.
Mbagathi Ridge, Karen (tel: 882 362).

Kichaka

Hand-stencilled textiles and clothes from T-shirts to caftans.
Kijabe Street (tel: 228 807/229 187).

Lenana Forest Centre

A fascinating gemstone and mineral workshop where you can watch the stones being cut and polished before you buy.
256 Collins Road, Karen (tel: 882 297).

The Spinner's Web

All sorts of fine natural fabrics and woven goods, from baskets to jumpers.
Kijabe Street (tel: 228 647).

Utamaduni

A good, if comparatively expensive centre for crafts. A percentage of the takings is donated to conservation charities. Dance displays every lunchtime.
Langata Road, near the Giraffe Centre and well sign-posted (tel: 212 852).

MOMBASA

The whole of Moi Avenue is lined with souvenir shops and galleries, while large sections of Moi Avenue and Nyerere Street have grown a second skin of small stalls. The best fabrics are to be found in Biashara Street. In the old town, particularly on Mbarak Hinawy Road, many of the fine old houses have now joined the souvenir trade. You stand a fighting chance of finding something a little different here, with ornate Lamu chests, Ethiopian silver and Arabic coffee sets alongside the normal carvings and bags.

Ali's Curio Market

Large, jazzy and colourful shop housed in the former Police Headquarters, built in 1898.
Opposite Fort Jesus, Old Town (tel: 312 647).

Bombolulu

A rehabilitation centre for the blind and handicapped who make jewellery, hand-printed cotton clothes and leather goods. The workshop tours and factory shop have become a major tourist attraction in their own right.
Malindi Road, 3km north of Mombasa town (tel: 471 704/473 571). Open: Monday to Friday, 7.30am–12.30pm and 2pm–5pm. The shop is open Monday to Saturday, 8am–5pm.

Labeka

A real notch above the other shops along Moi Avenue, with beautiful makonde carvings as well as antiques, including silver and amber jewellery.
Moi Avenue (tel: 312 232) and Beach Road (tel: 473 023).

NANYUKI

There is a great gathering of souvenir stalls around the Equator sign, just south of town, while the Mount Kenya Safari

Club (see page 72) houses some extremely up-market boutiques and galleries.

Cotton Culture

Outdo Stewart Granger and kit up in a leopard-print safari jacket.
Corner of Kenyatta Highway and Lumumba Road (tel: 32365).

The Spinners' and Weavers' Co-operative

Founded in 1977, to employ local women who spin, weave, dye, knit and sell a variety of products from rugs to jumpers and gossamer-light shawls.
In the grounds of the Presbyterian Church, Nyeri Road.

Spinner at the Nanyuki Spinners' and Weavers' Co-operative

MARKETS

The most extraordinary thing about Kenya's markets is the enormous number of brightly coloured plastic bowls and buckets on sale, looking from a distance like a toy shop gone haywire. In the large towns, there are permanent covered markets, with set stalls under barn-like roofs. But where you have more than three houses and a shop, a market will spring up once a week and people will trek in, on foot, by bus, *matatu* or in battered trucks, from miles around.

The market square is outlined by a row of dusty shops, made gay by blue and scarlet Bata and Coca Cola signs. In their gloomy depths, shelves groan

cluster in the doorways, drinking warm sodas. The butcher's shop, as dingy as the rest, is marked by a gaily painted cartoon pig. Under a shady tree, a rusty wheel proclaims the territory of the puncture repair man. Near by, an itinerant barber has set up shop with little more than a chair, a bowl of water and a pair of scissors. An old woman crouches behind a smoking brazier, turning her roasting cobs of corn.

under an extraordinary array of biscuits and car parts, text books and ageing tins of jam, while the young men

Anyone with something to sell just sets up shop, laying a cloth out on the ground to mark their space. On it, they heap mounds of clothes or piles of potatoes. One woman has arrived with two bucket-loads of oranges, another with a goat, a third is doing a roaring trade in recycled maize meal sacks and sandals made from car tyres. And always, somewhere in the general maelstrom, some hopeful person has laid out some beads and bangles, baskets or wooden animals, and squats beside them waiting for a tourist to arrive.

Kenya's markets are loud, brightly coloured and stuffed with everything from bananas to buckets

Entertainment

*T*here is a wide range of entertainment on offer in Nairobi, a reasonable array in Mombasa and Nyali, a small amount in Malindi, and virtually nothing elsewhere. Except in Nairobi, the local social life revolves almost exclusively around the bars. It is impossible to leave your lodge in the game parks and often difficult to get out of the more isolated beach resorts, so these hotels do try to arrange entertainment each evening, from occasional discos and barbecues to videos, lectures and the ubiquitous Masai dancers. If you are looking to rave around the clock, stay in Nairobi. To find out what's on, read the entertainment listings in *The Nation*.

CASINOS

NAIROBI
Casino de Paradise
Safari Park Hotel, Thika Road (tel: 802 493 or fax: 802 477).
Intercontinental Hotel
City Hall Way (tel: 335 550 or fax: 210 675).
International
Museum Hill (tel: 742 600).

MOMBASA
Florida Casino
Mama Ngina Drive (tel: 316 810).
International Casino
Oceanic Hotel, Light House Road (tel: 312 838).
International Casino
Leisure Lodge, Diani Beach (tel: 0127-2159).
Nyali Beach Hotel Casino (tel: 471 551).

MALINDI
There is a casino on Lamu Road (tel: 21104).

CINEMAS

As ever, the only real choice is in Nairobi, which has several good cinemas and numerous flea-pits. Prices in them all are a fraction of those in the West. If you have a car, try an evening at one of the two drive-ins; they are really good fun for weather-bound Europeans who have only ever seen them on the movies!

Most of the top Hollywood films make it into the main cinemas, along with an inexhaustible supply of Hindi movies. You may not understand these, but if you have never seen one, choose the one with the most lurid poster and grab the opportunity – they are a mind-blowing experience. For independent and 'foreign' films, you will need to go to the cultural institutes (see below).

NAIROBI
The Kenya Plaza, *Moi Avenue (tel: 226 981)*.
The Nairobi, *Aga Khan Walk (tel: 228 650)*.
Twentieth Century Fox, *Mama Ngina Street (tel: 227 957)*.
The Fox Drive-In, *Thika Road (tel: 802 293)*.
The Belle-Vue Drive-In, *Mombasa Road (tel: 558 112)*.

MOMBASA
There are four small cinemas: the **Kenya**, on Nkrumah Road; the **Lotus**, on Makadara Road; the **Majestic**, on Nehru Road; and **Moons**, on Khalifa Road.

CULTURAL CENTRES

The various national cultural centres, such as the British Council and Alliance Française, organise a range of activities from film shows to lectures and exhibitions. They are popular with residents and a good place to meet expats.

NAIROBI

Alliance Française, *ICEA Building, Kenyatta Avenue (tel: 340 054).*
American Cultural Centre, *National Bank Building, Harambee Avenue (tel: 337 877).*
British Council, *ICEA Building, Kenyatta Avenue (tel: 334 855).*
German Goethe Institute, *Maendeleo House, corner of Monrovia and Loita streets (tel: 224 640).*
Italian Cultural Institute, *Prudential Assurance Building, Wabera Street (tel: 220 278).*

MOMBASA

Alliance Française, *Freed Building, Moi Avenue (tel: 25048).*
British Council, *City House, Nyerere Avenue (tel: 23076).*

DHOW TRIPS

Several companies operate up-market tours in elegant *dhows* around Mombasa island. All, unfortunately, are priced in hard currency and are fairly expensive, but are still worthwhile. The operators will collect you from, and deliver you back to, your hotel. All are bookable through hotels, travel agents or direct.
Jahazi Marine
Two trips daily: the midday Discover Mombasa Cruise with stops for lunch and the floating craft-market; and Mombasa by Night, with sundowners on board, dinner at Bamburi Quarry

followed by visits to a casino and nightclub. *(Tel: 472 213/471 895.)*
Kenya Marineland *Dhows*
Three trips daily: in the morning, afternoon (with seafood lunch) and evening (with African meal and entertainment). The ticket includes free entry to Kenya Marineland. *(Tel: 485 248/886/7738.)*
Tamarind *Dhows*
Two trips daily: at lunchtime and at night. The evening cruise is an absolute must, a superbly romantic night under the stars in an elegantly carved *dhow*, with a gourmet lobster dinner served on board and dancing to a band overlooking the floodlit waterfront of Mombasa Old Town. *(Tel: 220 990 or fax: 314 226.)*

A pyramid of acrobats, one of the most popular ways to entertain resort guests

MUSIC AND DANCING

NAIROBI

Nairobi has a wide selection of discos and clubs from the sedate to the raucous. Be wary at all times of pickpockets.

Bubbles

Recently refurbished, this is one of the more up-market discos for the sophisticated palate. *Beside the International Casino, Museum Hill, off Westlands Road (tel: 742 600).*

The Cantina Club

Large club, with everything from barbecue and darts to discos, live music and floor shows with dancers and acrobats. The accent is on African music and food, and there are regular theme nights. *Wilson Airport Road, Langata (tel: 506 085).*

Florida 2000 and New Florida

Both very noisy, cheerful, popular and renowned pick-up joints, the party continues all night. *Florida 2000, Moi Avenue (tel: 334 892) and New Florida, Koinange Street (tel: 334 870/215 014).*

Brash and bright, Florida 2000 is Nairobi's favourite club

Simba Saloon Disco

Part of the famous Carnivore complex, so come out to eat zebra and stay on to bop. Live music on Wednesday (jazz), Friday (African music) and Sunday (soul). Carnivore is also one of the main venues for the few international groups coming into Kenya. *Carnivore, Langata Road (tel: 501 775).*

Sting

There is a piano bar in the early evenings which is followed by a disco late at night. *Safari Park Hotel (see under Casinos, page 154).*

Visions

Popular glitzy disco with video screens and a wide-ranging clientele. *Kimathi Street (tel: 323 331).*

Zanze Bar

Popular haunt of a young, fun-loving local crowd. *Kenya Cinema Plaza, Moi Avenue (tel: 222 532).*

THE COAST

Dancing is about the only sort of entertainment in plentiful supply along the coast. Mombasa and Malindi both have independent clubs, and almost every resort hotel has a disco at least one night a week. The catch is that many of them use the same travelling DJ, so keen dancers will be following him along the hotel strip and if you don't like his style, tough luck.

MOMBASA

Bora Bora, *Malindi Road, Nyali (tel: 485 076).*
New Florida Club, *Mama Ngina Drive (tel: 313 127).*
Toyz, *Biluchi Street, off Moi Avenue (tel: 229 658).*
These three are all a loud mix of disco music, light shows and carabet with Vegas-style showgirls in glittering bikinis.

MALINDI
Stardust Disco, *Lamu Road (tel: 20338)*.
Tropicana Club 28, *Lamu Road (tel: 20480)*.

Elsewhere in the country, the only dancing on offer will be in the local bars or at the occasional dinner-dance thrown by a local society.

THEATRE
There are three theatres in Nairobi and one in Mombasa, all churning out amateur productions of perennial favourites from all over the world.
Braeburn Theatre, *Litanga Road, Nairobi (tel: 567 901)*.
Kenya National Theatre, *Harry Thuku Road, Nairobi (tel: 220 536)*.
Phoenix Players, *Parliament Road, Nairobi (tel: 225 506)*.
Little Theatre Club, *Mnazi Moja Road, Mombasa (tel: 312 101)*.

TRIBAL DANCING
Real tribal dancing is virtually extinct these days, with even the traditionalist Masai more likely to be adapting the ancient steps to U2 or Bob Marley. You might find the real thing if you stray out into the very deepest depths of beyond, but it is unlikely. Dance displays are now almost the sole province of the hotels. Some coastal resorts provide dancers from the local Giriama tribe; most, no matter where they are, have a selection of resident Masai who leap for half an hour after dinner.

The Bomas of Kenya
Daily demonstrations of traditional African dance – noisy, colourful and great fun. All the dances are performed by a professional troupe and there is an accompanying programme which gives

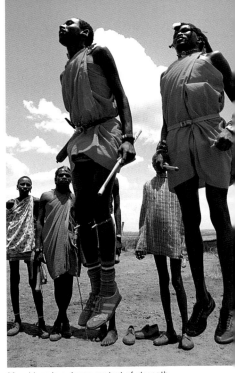
Masai leap in a dance contest of strength

some background.
Forest Edge Road, Langata (tel: 891 801). 10km southeast of Nairobi, off the Langata road. Weekdays, 2.30pm; weekends, 3.30pm; and some evenings. Admission charge.

Mountain Rock Lodge
Displays of dance from a range of tribes, performed by an enthusiastic local team, arranged on request. Ticket charge. This is a completely whacky experience, with an elderly gentleman with a huge hat and a vast smile pumping an accordion, and energetic audience participation to the traditional Kikuyu strains of *The Last Waltz*. Unforgettable.
PO Box 333, Nanyuki (tel: 0176-62625/98). Between Naro Moru and Nanyuki, on the Mt Kenya ring road.

Children

*T*he vast majority of Kenya's population is under 15 years of age. For the most part, however, African families are too poor to pay for entertainment for their children; instead they start work in the fields or at home alongside their parents almost as soon as they can walk. As a result, there are few attractions specifically designed for children.

On the other hand, the whole country is a giant playground, with an excellent climate, wide open spaces to run around in, and endless fascinating creatures to look at. There are chances to ride horses and camels, swim, tickle giant tortoises and hold a python. The Africans love small children and will happily include them in any activity. Wherever they go, your children will find an instant swarm of friends, even if they cannot speak the same language.

SUPPLIES
You can buy all the basics, from steriliser to nappies and baby foods in any town. What you won't find is choice, recognisable labels, and instant, throwaway options, so take a large supply of disposable nappies and baby food. Hats, sunblock, sandals and travel sickness pills are essentials.

El Molo children playing on the shore of Lake Turkana

BABYSITTING
The chief problem is keeping your children safe. They will be enthralled by their surroundings without any concept of the unfamiliar dangers and you must ensure that they don't eat peculiar insects or drink stream water given to them by a kindly local mum. Most resort hotels have babysitting facilities, available during the day and in the evening, although few have children's playgrounds or facilities. Most resorts have an early children's sitting for dinner and expect them to be banished after that.

CHILDREN ON THE COAST
Most of the organised attractions, such as crocodile farms and snake parks, are to be found in the Nyali area, north of Mombasa (see pages 110–11). The resort hotels all have swimming pools and there is easy access to the beach. Do not let children near the sea unattended, as there are sometimes strong currents as well as peculiar sea creatures from urchins upwards. Older children will love a chance to go snorkelling on the coral reef, and some of the resorts have facilities for windsurfing and other water sports. Discos are rarely suitable for teenagers.

Swimming in the sea is great fun under careful supervision

CHILDREN ON SAFARI

Taking small infants on safari is probably foolhardy. They won't know why they are there and the grizzling will drive you insane. Older children (five and over) will love it. The normal style of minibus trip is really not suitable for children. The very long hours of driving over dusty roads in the company of strange adults would be hell for parents and children alike.

To cut down on the driving, stick to one game park. If you have the money, fly in, stay at a lodge or tented camp with a swimming pool, and book game-viewing trips through the hotel. An alternative would be to look at the custom-made private safaris. All children love camping and eating round a bonfire. If there are several of you, it need not be astronomically expensive, and you effectively have a private holiday with a staff to help with the practicalities. You could even hire a nanny for the duration.

Take plenty of things to keep the children entertained on car journeys and during the heat of the day. If they are old enough, consider setting them a project such as a travel diary. It will keep them occupied, focus their interest and help them remember an amazing experience.

Sport

*T*he Kenyans are not a particularly sporting nation. For most, the normal grind of everyday life involves too much exercise for them to see any further activity as either necessary or pleasurable. Nevertheless, there is a wide base of sporting activity across the country, with football and boxing keen favourites among the young. In particular, Kenya has achieved international status in athletics, with a stream of superb middle- and long-distance runners.

The Asian community keeps up a tradition of cricket and hockey, some of the wealthier Africans have taken up golf, racing and polo, but on the whole, the more expensive sports have remained the province of Europeans and tourists.

Kenya has two large sports venues, both in Nairobi and seriously underused – the Nyayo Stadium on Uhuru Highway, and the vast Moi International Stadium on Thika Road, built by the Chinese for the 1987 Pan-Africa Games, and capable of holding 60,000 people.

To find out what is on in the way of spectator sports, read *The Nation* sports diary on Saturdays. For participatory sports, see below, or ask at your hotel reception desk.

AERIAL SPORTS

Although many Kenyans use small planes, relatively few indulge in other aerial sports. Ballooning is one of the

Football is taken very seriously, at every level from village to international

great – and expensive – treats on offer (see page 139). There is a small gliding club at Mweiga, in the Central Highlands, whose members will take up visitors on an *ad hoc* basis. Meanwhile, the great cliffs and thermals of the Rift Valley are attracting world class hang-gliders, starry-eyed at the prospect of record-breaking flights.

The Aero Club of East Africa, *Wilson Airport (PO Box 40813), Nairobi (tel: 501 772).*

FOOTBALL
More than any other, this is Kenya's national sport, played at every level from village to the hotly contested national league. The two top teams are AFC Leopards and Gor Mahia, while the national team, the Harambee Stars, have proved winners in Africa, but still have a low ranking worldwide.

The Kenya Football Federation, *Nyayo Stadium, Uhuru Highway (PO Box 40234), Nairobi (tel: 226 138).*

GOLF
Golf has been popular in Kenya since the 1930s, but it is only recently that people have begun to regard the country as a suitable place for a golfing holiday. There are six high-quality, 18-hole courses in and around Nairobi, of which the finest, without question, is at the Windsor Golf and Country Club. This tough 7,400-yard course has been built to international standards in hopes of attracting the top professional circuit.

Outside the Nairobi area, there are 10 courses in the Rift Valley and Central Highlands, often with spectacular settings. Most other main towns have a nine-hole course, many of them built by local farmers during the colonial period. Most are open to casual visitors, with

Golf is popular, with courses scattered liberally across the Central Highlands

reasonable green fees.

For more information contact the **Kenya Golf Union**, *Muthaiga (PO Box 49609), Nairobi (tel: 763 898). The* **Windsor Golf and Country Club** *is 13km from Nairobi city centre, off Garden Estate Road (PO Box 45587), (tel: 802 206/8/10 or fax: 802 188).* **UTC** *and* **Let's Go Travel Ltd** *(see page 189) will organise golfing safaris for anyone interested.*

HIKING
Much of the best hiking in Kenya is high altitude, with the summit of Mount Kenya as the great goal. Several other ranges, including Mount Elgon, the Aberdares, and the Cherenganis offer brilliant mountain walking.

The other great way to do some serious hiking is on a walking safari through game country. There are several varieties on offer, using trucks or camels as back-up.

See also pages 76–9, or contact **The Mountain Club of Kenya**, *Wilson Airport (PO Box 45741), Nairobi (tel: 501 747). For walking safaris, see page 143.*

HORSE-RACING

Races are held at the Nairobi Racecourse on most Sunday afternoons, except in August and September.

Nairobi Racecourse, *Ngong Road, 10km southwest of the city centre (tel: 566 108). Admission free to the Silver Ring.*

Jockey Club of Kenya, *PO Box 40373, Nairobi (tel: 561 002).*

MOTOR-RACING

The **Safari Rally** is a four-day rally held annually over the Easter weekend. This great endurance feat, covering some 4,000km of Kenya's awful roads and tracks, has become one of the main events on the international rally circuit. The gruelling **Rhino Charge**, held annually on the first weekend in June, raises money for rhino conservation. Participants donate vast sums (minimum 750,000 shillings) to drive as fast as possible from one point to another with little regard for terrain. The start point and route are kept secret until shortly before the race, but are revealed in *What's On* or local radio.

The **East Africa Motor Sports Club**, *Mombasa Road (PO Box 42786), Nairobi (tel: 822 843).*

Safari Rally Ltd, *Nyaku House (PO Box 59483), Nairobi (tel: 720 382).*

WATER SPORTS

FISHING

Deep-sea fishing

Kenya has some of the greatest sports-fishing grounds in the world, and a nine-month season from August to May. The main species found here include blue, black and striped marlin, swordfish, sailfish, sharks, kingfish, dorado, barracuda and wahoo. All operators are increasingly encouraging a tag and release policy to help conservation and scientific research.

Hemingways, *PO Box 267, Watamu, 25km south of Malindi (tel: 32624 or fax: 32256).* The single greatest deep-sea fishing centre in Kenya.

James Adcock Fishing Ltd, *Mtwapa Creek (PO Box 95693), Nyali, Mombasa (tel: 485 527).*

Pemba Channel Fishing and Diving Club, *PO Box 86952, Mombasa (tel: 313 744 or fax: 316 875).* Based at Shimoni with trips to Kisite Island (see page 112).

Freshwater fishing

The mountain streams of the Aberdares, the Mau Escarpment and the Cherenganis, provide excellent fly-fishing opportunities, especially for trout. Lake Victoria is an excellent centre for game-fishing with tiger fish and Nile perch among other species. With the exception of the exclusive Rusinga Island and Mfangano Island resorts (see page 92), there are no organised facilities. You can hire equipment cheaply through the Naro Moru River Lodge (see page 77), the Mount Kenya Safari Club (see page 72) and Let's Go Travel Ltd (see page 189).

Licences are required, available at low cost from the **Fisheries Dept**, *PO Box 58187, Nairobi (tel: 743 579).*

The **Dagoretti Trout and Salmon Flies Factory** is a major manufacturer and exporter of fly-fishing lures. Choose from an enormous range at a fraction of their Western price. Take a local guide for security in the area. *Kikuyu Road, Nairobi (tel: 569 790).*

SWIMMING

There are few public swimming pools, but most good hotels have one. Do not swim in lakes and rivers, as many have bilharzia and crocodiles.

Windsurfing is one of many watersports on offer at Diani Beach

Access to the sea is easy along the coast. South from Mombasa, there is a lot of seaweed close to the shore. Never let children swim unattended as there can be strong waves and currents as well as nasties, such as sea urchins, on the bottom.

Diving and snorkelling

The snorkelling is superb and most coastal hotels have equipment for hire. Access to the reefs is usually by glass-bottomed boats. Be very careful not to damage the coral.

You need to be trained in order to dive. If qualified, take your certificates, or be prepared to take a test. Most of the diving here is drift diving, with a normal maximum depth of 30m and visibility of around 25–35m. The season is from September to April. The best sites are in the marine parks, especially in the Malindi/Watamu area. There is a park admission fee on top of the boat and equipment hire.

For a full range of recognised courses and diving equipment try:

Barracuda Diving School, *c/o Sevrin Sea Lodge, Mombasa (tel: 485 001)*. Based at several hotels in Mombasa, Nyali and Watamu.
Hemingways and **Pemba Channel Fishing and Diving Club** (see under Deep-sea fishing on page 162).
One Earth Safaris and Diving, *PO Box 82234, Mombasa (tel: 471 771 or fax: 471 349)*. Diving safaris based at the Reef Hotels in Nyali, Diani Beach and Shimoni, and Pemba Island.
Scuba Diving Kenya Ltd, *PO Box 160, Watamu (tel: 32099 or fax: 32430)*. Two centres at the Blue Bay Village, Watamu, and the Driftwood Club, Malindi.

OTHER WATER SPORTS

Windsurfing, paragliding, and water-skiing are available at many coastal resorts. Check at your hotel's reception desk.
Harald Geier's Windsurfing School, *Surf and Safaris Ltd, Turtle Bay Beach Hotel (PO Box 168), Watamu (tel: 32622 or fax: 32268)*.

Food and Drink

*I*t comes as a surprise to find Kenya as something of a gourmet paradise. Africa as a whole is not noted for the quality of its food, but Kenya has one massive advantage – it can produce almost everything from fine beef to a wide variety of seafood, from strawberries and apples to bananas, passion fruit and papaya. The quality and range of the superb tropical fruits is the single greatest treat the country has to offer.

As each new wave of people has entered the country, they have brought their traditional foods with them. The result is an enormous range of cuisines, from traditional African fare to English pies and puddings. Swahili and Indian dishes have been absorbed as local standards, and pizza, pasta and hamburgers are coming up from behind. Meanwhile, the international tourist trade has quietly transformed standards, bringing in foreign chefs who can rival the best French kitchens. Most restaurants have at least one vegetarian option.

Food tends to come in enormous quantities – either in set meals of several courses, or on the groaning buffet tables that have become a Kenyan hallmark. These can be found in most hotels and restaurants, and offer amazing value, as-much-as-you-can-eat feasts for ludicrously low prices.

Prices

The quality and prices of restaurants fall into two distinct categories. The lower end is made up of a large number of roadside stalls and tiny hotels. These are all incredibly cheap. The upper end covers all those restaurants considered by locals to be suitable for tourists, from coffee bars to gourmet restaurants. Even here, food is not expensive, although it will be on a par with American and cheaper European rates. All taxes and a service charge are usually included in the bill.

In the listings below, the following symbols have been used to indicate the average cost per person of a full meal, not including alcohol:

S = Under 250 shillings
SS = 250–500 shillings
SSS = 500–1000 shillings
SSSS = Above 1000 shillings

WHERE TO EAT

There are many excellent restaurants in Nairobi and Mombasa, but away from these centres there is often little choice. In the game parks, you have to eat at your lodge. It takes some effort to move around at night from many of the coastal resort hotels, and in the smaller towns you will find one reasonable restaurant, usually in the old colonial hotel, and a selection of more or less hygienic hotels, roadside and market stalls, serving African food or fish-and-chips at rock bottom prices. These can be fun for an evening with a difference, but while the food is edible, you will rarely get a good meal. None are listed here as there are so many and they change so frequently. Ask hotel staff or your driver for a suggestion, or choose the most hygienic.

The following list makes no attempt to cover every destination, and also ignores those hotels which have you trapped, although many of them serve excellent food. It concentrates instead on those places that are really worth making an effort to visit.

NAIROBI

African Heritage SS
Traditional African food with craft displays and live African bands.
Kenyatta Avenue (tel: 333 157) and Libra House, Mombasa Road, 7km from the city centre (tel: 554 547).

Bobbe's Bistro SSSS
Intimate, friendly restaurant serving wonderful French food. Popular with expats, so book early.
Koinange Street (tel: 224 945/336 952).

Carnivore SSS
So popular it has become a tourist attraction. A massive barbecue pit which offers a wide variety of meat from beef to zebra, warthog or impala. There is also a snack bar serving vegetarian food. Reservations advisable.
Off Langata Road, 6km from the city centre, signposted opposite the Kobil garage (tel: 501 709/775).

Dhaba SS
Brilliant North Indian restaurant decorated with murals of the Punjab.
Keekorok Road, at top end of Tom Mboya Street (tel: 334 862).

Iqbal Hotel S
Very cheap and cheerful, serving traditional African and Indian food.
Latema Road, near the Odeon Cinema (tel: 20914).

Mandy's S
Everything from pizza to hamburgers or curry at bargain prices.
Koinange Street (tel: 20193).

Perfect service and fresh fruit cocktails add to the ideal lazy holiday

Norfolk Hotel SSSS
Nairobi's oldest and most atmospheric hotel, with a range of restaurants from snacks on the **Delamere Terrace** to buffets and carvery in the **Delamere Restaurant** to full blown, mouth-watering à la carte *haute cuisine* in the **Ibis Grill**. Reservations advisable.
Harry Thuku Road (tel: 335 422).

Le Restaurant SSSS
One of Nairobi's finest restaurants, with mouth-watering food and seafood specialities. Booking essential.
Nairobi Racecourse, Ngong Road (tel: 561 002).

The Tamarind SSSS
Wonderful, very classy seafood restaurant. Reservations advisable.
National Bank Building, Aga Khan Walk, off Harambee or Haile Selassie Avenues (tel: 338 959).

COMMON AFRICAN DISHES

With the exception of the nomadic pastoralists who lived traditionally on blood and milk, most of the inland tribes have a diet high in carbohydrates, with plenty of vegetables and little meat or sugar. When an animal is slaughtered, every scrap is used, and there are plenty of recipes for offal, blood sausages, and even brains, although you rarely see these on a restaurant menu. Near the large lakes, fish (mainly tilapia) is the major source of protein.

Nyama choma: literally roast meat, usually goat, cooked over an open fire.
Sukuma wiki: kale, introduced by the Europeans as cattle fodder, was adopted by the locals as a cheap, nourishing source of vitamins. It often appears in restaurants as 'spinach'.
Matoke: mashed green plantains
Irio: a vegetable mash of peas, maize and potatoes, usually served with a meat stew or tomato sauce.
Githeri: vegetable hot-pot with almost everything in it – maize, red beans, potatoes, carrots, *sukuma wiki*, tomatoes, onions and, sometimes, meat!

Left: Kenyan women grading peanuts
Below: Villagers hard at work crushing grain in the traditional way

On the coast, the key ingredients of typical Swahili food are fish (whether barracuda, snapper or lobster), rice, coconut and lime. To these are added a variety of spices from chillies to ginger, creating a delicious, fresh, piquant taste very similar to the food of Goa – which is directly opposite, on the far side of the Indian Ocean.
Ugali: a thick maize meal porridge, normally eaten with a vegetable stew or meat gravy. With the onset of the drought, this has become more of a luxury.

The Toona Tree SSS
Eclectic menu and a good atmosphere.
International Casino, Museum HIll
(tel: 742 600).

La Trattoria SS
Excellent traditional Italian restaurant.
Corner of Wabera/Kaunda streets
(tel: 340855).

Where to drink
Delamere Terrace, Norfolk Hotel
(see page 165).

Thorn Tree Café
Famous for the travellers' message board
around a huge acacia thorn tree.
New Stanley Hotel, Kimathi Street
(tel: 333 233).

The Zanze Bar
Popular spot with a happy hour and live
jazz. Entry charge in the evenings.
5th Floor, Kenya Cinema Plaza, Moi
Avenue (tel: 222 532).

Above: the famous Thorn Tree Café, in front
of the New Stanley Hotel

CENTRAL HIGHLANDS
The Kentmere Club SSS
Superb range of international gourmet
food, but with an accent on French
cuisine. Set in beautiful gardens.
Tigoni, Limuru, PO Box 39508, Nairobi
(tel: 0154-41053). 30km from Nairobi on
the old Naivasha Road.

Mount Kenya Safari Club SSSS
Only members or overnight guests can eat
here, but the expense is almost worth it
for the fabulous food alone.
PO Box 35, Nanyuki (tel: 22960 or fax:
22754). Booking via Lonrho (see page 171).
Turn off near the Nanyuki Equator sign.

RIFT VALLEY
La Belle Inn SS
Excellent *nouvelle cuisine* at reasonable
rates, plus a first-class bakery.
Moi Avenue, Naivasha (tel: 20116).

THE COAST

The vast majority of good restaurants in Mombasa and Malindi are in the resort hotels, most of which have a coffee shop, and a couple of restaurants.

Among those with the best food are the **Indian Ocean Beach Club** on Diani Beach, and the **Nyali Beach Hotel**, Nyali.

MOMBASA
Recoda SS

Cheap and extremely popular Swahili restaurant in the heart of the old town. Open evenings only.
Nyeri Street (old town).

Shenai SSS

Delightful Indian restaurant with wonderful food and an ornate, incense-filled atmosphere. No alcohol.
Off Moi Avenue, behind the Hotel Splendid (tel: 312 492).

The Tamarind SSSS

Superb seafood restaurant perched on a clifftop with views across to Mombasa Old Town. If this still isn't romantic enough for you, take their dinner and dancing *dhow* cruise (see page 155).
Nyali Beach, 6km north of Mombasa town (tel: 471 729).

La Terrazza SS

Good value Italian restaurant.
Oceanic Hotel, Mbuyini Road (tel: 311 191).

Where to drink

Hard Rock Café

The coolest and most exclusive of the local crowd hang out here.
Electricity House, Nkrumah Road (tel: 222 221).

Relaxing at Amboseli Safari Lodge

Hunters Bar

An air-conditioned mecca for laid-back locals and heat-blasted tourists.
Hunters Hotel, Jomo Kenyatta Avenue (tel: 490 500).

Istanbul Bar

A noisy, lively bar which doubles as a pick-up point.
Moi Avenue.

MALINDI
Degli-Artisti SSS

Massive Italian trattoria and pizzeria with good but relatively pricey food, very geared up for the tourist trade.
Lamu Road (tel: 20710).

The Driftwood Club SS

Laid-back resort restaurant serving seafood, barbecues and good value set meals in the main dining room.
Signposted off the Mombasa Road, at the southern end of the town, PO Box 63 (tel: 20155).

LAMU
The Bush Garden S and Hapa Hapa SS

Two small, very good restaurants, both of which specialise in Swahili-style seafood.
On the sea front.

Peponi Hotel SSS

Upmarket resort hotel on the beach, away from Lamu Town, with excellent international cuisine, including, as always in Lamu, wonderful seafood.
Shela Beach (tel: 29).

Where to drink

Lamu is 'dry' and the only places to get a drink are in the more up-market hotels such as **Peponi Hotel** in Shela and **Petley's Inn** in Lamu Town.

DRINK

Drinking is very important in Kenyan social life, whether it is sodas or beer. Both are widely available and cheap. Africans generally prefer their drinks warm, so specify that you want a cold one (*baridi*) when ordering.

There are two brands of lager, Tusker and White Cap, both of which also come in Premium and Export versions. Both are very drinkable and Tusker, at least, has made it on to the chic international menus of the European wine bars. The adventurous could also try the local African beers, *muratina*, made from fermented sugar cane, and *buzaa*, made from fermented maize meal.

Wine-drinking is not recommended. Kenya does produce some wine, the best of which is from Naivasha. Both red and white are pleasant plonk, but relatively expensive. Papaya wine, on the other hand, *is* cheap, but this is the best that can be said about it. The imported wines stocked at the better restaurants tend to be supermarket labels with château-bottled, vintage prices.

Few people can afford spirits, as imported drinks have astronomic taxes slapped on to them. Ever inventive, the country does produce local versions of whisky, gin, vodka and brandy, which are reasonable if drowned with a mixer. There are also two local liqueurs; Kenya Cane, a potent brew of cane spirit, and Kenya Gold, a pleasant coffee-based liqueur. At the bottom end of the market, *changa* covers a variety of home-distilled spirits which vary from stripping your stomach to making you blind.

In the better establishments, the coffee and tea are both excellent. Down market, tea comes as Indian-style *chai*, with the milk and huge amounts of sugar all brewed up together.

Hotels and Accommodation

*K*enya has a wide range of accommodation from glorious luxury hotels to sleazy tin shacks and brothels with a couple of long-stay rooms. Most of the best are owned by a handful of chains, such as Block, Lonrho and Sarova, who all have a variety of Nairobi hotels, coastal resorts and game lodges.

The chief problem is that prices for the quality hotels are listed in US dollars, with hefty additions for non-Kenyans (see **Prices**, page 186). While the package operators negotiate substantial discounts, rack rates for non-residents are equivalent to those in the West. This may be just, but with many more affordable 3-star hotels currently upgrading, there is a dearth of decent mid-range accommodation for independent travellers.

The fullest list of hotels in the country can be found in *What's On* magazine.

Business hotels

Nairobi has plenty of excellent 5-star hotels, run by the main chains, which double up to cater for international business trade and the luxury tourist market. In Mombasa, most businessmen stay in the resort hotels in nearby Nyali Beach. All have a full range of services. Expect to pay upwards of US$150 per night.

Mid-range and old colonial hotels

Nairobi is the only city with a reasonable range of good quality, affordable hotels. The best are the **Fairview, Jacaranda, Ambassadeur**, the **Boulevard** and **Mayfair Hotel**. In Mombasa, there is only one real contender, the **Manor**.

Elsewhere, every town across the country has one old colonial hotel. In

Chalet accommodation at Amboseli Lodge

At the higher end of the accommodation spectrum, Scorpio Villas swimming pool, Malindi

many instances, it is still the finest on offer. With the odd exception, such as the luxurious (and expensive) **Norfolk Hotel** in Nairobi, most have sunk back into atmospheric decay. They can be a little spartan, but they are usually spotlessly clean and perfectly comfortable. Most are privately owned, and there is no central listing, but ask any local.

Many 3-star establishments cater primarily for locals, so have not bothered with non-resident rates. Expect to pay US$30–50 a night.

Cheap and cheerful

There is at least one cheap hotel in even the tiniest of towns, but quality ranges from spartan to dire. Always ask to check the room before booking in.

Nairobi has a good Youth Hostel, YMCA and YWCA and several clean, comfortable budget hotels. On the coast, there are one or two good cheap hotels in central Mombasa, but most budget travellers head for Tiwi Beach, which has excellent self-catering accommodation.

There are no budget hotels in the game parks, so you are, effectively, restricted to cheap camping safaris (see pages 142–3).

Prices range from 100 to 500 shillings.

CENTRAL BOOKING

African Tours and Hotels, PO Box 30471, Nairobi (tel: 336 858 or fax: 218 109).

Alliance Hotels, PO Box 49839, Nairobi (tel: 220 149 or fax: 219 212).

Block Hotels, PO Box 40075, Nairobi (tel: 540 780 or fax: 340 541).

The Conservation Corporation, PO Box 74957 (tel: 750 298; fax: 746 826).

Hilton Hotels, PO Box 30624, Nairobi (tel: 334 000).

Lonrho Hotels, PO Box 58581, Nairobi (tel: 216 940 or fax: 216 796).

Prestige Hotels, PO Box 74888, Nairobi (tel: 338 084; fax: 217 278).

Sarova Hotels, PO Box 30680, Nairobi (tel: 333 248 or fax: 211 472).

Serena Hotels, PO Box 48690, Nairobi (tel: 710 511; fax: 718 000)

OUT OF TOWN

Coastal resorts

From Malindi, right down to the
southern end of Diani beach, more and
more resort hotels are springing up. Most
are 4- or 5-star and, with the exception
of a few early constructions, have similar,
attractive architecture – a large central
building with *makute* (coconut) thatch,
surrounded by comfortable cottages
sprawling out across landscaped gardens.

Most resorts have luxurious pools as well
as access to the beach

They all have beach frontage and
swimming pools, and offer a variety of
entertainments from tribal dancing to
watersports. Most are geared towards the
package trade and all-in prices, though
the operators are very competitive.

Check before booking who the main
operators are, as the different
nationalities tend to book into different
hotels (one for the Germans, one for the
Italians, etc). The occasional lost soul
can spend a lonely holiday unable to
communicate with anyone round them.
Prices are about the same as in the game
lodges.

Game lodges

All Kenya's main game parks offer a
variety of up-market lodges. Those
within the gates are obviously more
convenient, as staying outside the park
may involve an hour's bumpy drive
before you get into the reserve. On the
other hand, many lodges on the fringes
have created private game sanctuaries
which act as extensions of the park
proper, and have one or two real
bonuses. On private land, you can go out
on guided walks or rides and night
drives. Many of the lodges have also
created artificial waterholes and salt-
licks, and even bait for leopards, so that
you have unparalleled game viewing
from the comfort of the verandah.

Most of the lodges are low, sprawling
buildings set in bright flower gardens.
They have you captive and consequently
do their best to arrange for a wide variety
of meals and entertainments, from
filmshows to the ubiquitous Masai
dancers. You spend the midday heat
back at base, so choose a lodge with a
swimming pool. Some, such as the Voi
Safari Lodge, on a cliff face above the
vast Tsavo plains, have quite spectacular

Camping is one of the most exciting ways to feel the true call of the bush

settings. Into this category, too, come the so-called 'tree' hotels, such as Treetops and Shimba Hills.

For this level of accommodation expect to pay upwards of US$150 a day.

Permanent tented camps

In many ways, these tented camps are very similar to the game lodges, and cost as much. They were designed to cater for those who believe that a safari is not 'real' unless you sleep under canvas. However, they are a long way from the dream of a night under the stars in the middle of nowhere. In most, the tents have hard roofs, to protect the fragile canvas from the sun. They also have soft beds, electric light and fully fitted private bathrooms. The tents are all on permanent pitches in landscaped grounds, and there is always at least one bar and restaurant and often a pool.

Private ranches

As yet, there are fewer than a dozen private ranches in Kenya open to tourists, although the concept is growing. They are all very different, from the 16,188-hectare **Lewa Downs** cattle ranch and rhino sanctuary near Isiolo, and **Lokitela**, a 364-hectare intensive dairy farm on the slopes of Mount Elgon, to the Swahili-style **Indian Ocean Lodge**, near Malindi, or **Olerai**, a magnificent 'Happy Valley' mansion near Lake Naivaska. You live as one of the family, meet deeply knowledgeable local people, get a chance to explore the working farms, and can still have a complete range of normal safari activities, either in the private game sanctuaries or in nearby national parks.

Prices range upwards from about US$100 a day. Booking through Bush Homes or Let's Go Travel Ltd (see page 189).

On Business

*K*enya's whole economic policy is based on two key factors – a crucial shortage of foreign currency, and rampant unemployment and urban drift. Most of the country's efforts since independence have been aimed at creating a broad-based local industry, using local raw materials where possible. This cuts down on the need to import and opens up new export markets, thus saving and creating foreign currency and providing local jobs.

Foreign investment is actively sought in most areas. The process of setting up a non-resident company is complicated, with numerous forms and permits, but hefty incentives are available, especially if you go into partnership with locals, create real training opportunities or set up shop in rural areas. In recent years, a foreign exchange auction has allowed people with large amounts of foreign currency to buy shillings at rates significantly better than the official bank rate.

Foreign companies will have no difficulty in bringing in key personnel from abroad, but are strongly encouraged to employ Kenyans, at all levels. There are many semi-skilled workers eager for work at low wages, but finding highly skilled technicians and managers locally can be difficult.

In theory, it is possible to repatriate both your profits and your initial investment, but in practice, it can be an unwieldy process with long delays and high taxes. There are also rules that ensure that foreign currency payments for exports do not go straight into an overseas bank.

THE NETWORK

It is easy to gain access to almost anyone in Kenya as long as you are tapped into the right grapevine. Newly arrived expats and aid workers are usually 'broken in'

either by their predecessor or other members of staff. The short-term visitor should take advantage of reciprocal agreements between clubs and service clubs, such as Rotary or Lions. Almost all influential businessmen in Kenya belong either to these or the old country clubs. If you are not a member, head for the main business drinking haunts, the terrace of the Norfolk Hotel, Nairobi, or the Manor Hotel, Mombasa.

BUSINESS HOURS

Monday to Friday, 8am–1pm and 2pm–5pm. Some private businesses also work from 8.30am–12.30pm on Saturdays.

BUSINESS ETIQUETTE

Make an appointment to see people before you arrive, and reconfirm it shortly before the meeting. Punctuality is expected of you, but don't always expect it in return. A suit and tie is normal business wear. Women should dress smartly, but need not indulge in power dressing. Given the status of most women in Kenya, they are likely to have a hard time convincing many African men of their authority anyway.

Take plenty of business cards and hand them out liberally. Shake hands with everyone at each meeting and parting, it is considered a sign of trust and goodwill. A bottle of Scotch is also a guaranteed ice-breaker, except among the teetotal Asian and Muslim communities. If things go well, you are likely to be invited out, or home, for a meal, so take some suitable small gifts.

Some local businessmen are amazingly efficient, but with many, reaching an agreement can be a long and frustrating process, with many smiles and promises and little action. Always keep an eye open for the hidden agenda and be prepared, in some instances, for the goodwill and the necessary permits to be expensive.

CONFERENCES

Nairobi is the unofficial business capital of central and east Africa, and as such, is geared up for handling major conferences. Elsewhere, the country is only really suitable for small groups who wish to work in an informal atmosphere. There are no major exhibition facilities.

Kenyatta International Conference Centre, City Square, PO Box 30746, Nairobi (tel: 332 383 or fax: 220 349). The only really large conference facility in Kenya, this 28-storey (105m high) building has a central auditorium which can hold up to 4,000 people, and facilities for smaller groups. In central Nairobi, it is within easy walking distance of most major business hotels.

The **Intercontinental**, **Windsor Golf** and **Safari Park** hotels in Nairobi can handle conferences for up to 200, while many other hotels across the country can cater for between 30 and 75 delegates (see central booking addresses on page 171) and the private ranches are ideal for small gatherings (see page 173).

BUSINESS MEDIA

For local business information read the daily newspaper *The Nation* and the weekly news magazine, *Weekly Review*. To keep up with events abroad, **CNN** broadcasts through the night on KTN TV channel, and both the **BBC World Service** and the **Voice of America** are accessible. *Time* and *Newsweek* magazines are widely sold in Nairobi and Mombasa.

Major international newspapers normally arrive between two days and a week after publication.

SECRETARIAL SERVICES

Nairobi
Computrain Secretarial Services, 5th Floor, Nanak House, Kimathi Street (tel: 221 882/214 529).
Directors Secretaries, 1st Floor, Fedha Towers, Muindi Mbingu Street (tel: 225 589/222697 or fax: 338 113).
Executive Business Centre Ltd, Finance House, Loita Street (tel: 338 041/338 045 or fax: 338 072).

Mombasa
Mombasa Secretarial Services, Social Security House, Nkrumah Road (tel: 311 423).

TRANSLATION SERVICES
Computrain Secretarial Services (see under Secretarial Services).
Translation services for Russian, German and French. They also offer computers for hire.

COMMUNICATIONS
See **Post** on page 187 and **Telephones** on pages 188–9.

FURTHER INFORMATION
Investment Promotion Centre, PO Box 55704, Nairobi (tel: 221 401 or telex: 25460).

Practical Guide

CONTENTS

ARRIVING

By air

Nairobi is the main air travel centre for East Africa, with regular scheduled flights by many airlines from around the world and is the best place in Africa for discounted tickets. Some international scheduled services fly into Mombasa airport, but this is mainly used by the charter companies. The state airline, Kenya Airways, runs regular services to some 30 destinations worldwide.

The Thomas Cook Network locations (pages 188–9) will offer airline ticket re-routing and revalidation, other travel-booking services and emergency assistance free of charge to MasterCard cardholders and travellers who have purchased travel tickets from Thomas Cook.

Airline Offices

Kenya Airways
Barclays Plaza, Loita Street, PO Box 41010, Nairobi (tel: 229 291; reservations: 210 771; fax: 336 252); and Jomo Kenyatta International Airport (tel: 822 171/822 288).
Electricity House, Mombasa (tel: 221251) and Moi Airport, Mombasa (tel: 433 211). There are also offices in Malindi (tel: 20237) and Kisumu (tel: 44056).

Air France
2nd Floor, International House, Mama Ngina Street, PO Box 30159, Nairobi (tel: 217 501/2/3; fax: 217 517); and Jomo Kenyatta International Airport (tel: 822 202).

Alitalia
Ground Floor, Lonrho House, Standard Street, PO Box 40097, Nairobi (tel: 224 362/3/4; fax: 337 439); and Jomo Kenyatta Airport (tel: 822 351).

British Airways
11th Floor, International House, City Hall Way, PO Box 45050, Nairobi (tel: 334 440/334 362; flight information 215 884); and Jomo Kenyatta International Airport (tel: 822 555).

KLM
Fedha Towers, Muindi Mbingi Street, PO Box 49239, Nairobi (tel: 332 673/7); and Jomo Kenyatta International Airport (tel: 822 376).

Lufthansa
9th Floor, AM Bank House, University Way, PO Box 30320, Nairobi (tel: 335 819/226 271; fax: 335 451/222 161); and Jomo Kenyatta International Airport (tel: 822 400/1).
For other airline addresses, see the phone book or _What's On_ magazine.

Airports
Jomo Kenyatta International
A duty-free shop is available on arrival and departure, with 24-hour banking in the arrivals hall. Kenya Airways buses run to and from the City Terminal on Loita Street; most hotels organise airport transfers; and there are plenty of taxis. _Off Mombasa Road, PO Box 19001, Nairobi (tel: 822 111). 15km southeast of the city centre._

Moi International
There are 24-hour banking and duty-free facilities on arrival and departure. Many offices open only for flights. There is a regular public bus into the city, but most tourist hotels are not on the island. Ask your hotel for transport or take a taxi. _Off Nairobi Road, PO Box 98498, Mombasa (tel: 433 211). 13km west of the city centre._

Customs
Currency
There is no limit on the amount of foreign currency you can bring in or take out. It is illegal to import or export Kenyan shillings. You can reconvert any leftover cash as long as you have exchange receipts to cover the amount.

Drugs
There are very stiff penalties against drug dealing. Do not attempt it. If you take drugs for medical purposes also carry a letter of authority from your doctor.

Duty-free allowances
Tobacco 227g, or 200 cigarettes or 50 cigars; 1 litre of alcohol (wine or spirits) per person; and 0.6 litres of perfume.

Departure tax
There is a small departure tax, payable in shillings, even on domestic flights. On international departures, non-residents must pay a tax of US$20 or equivalent in hard currency cash. Travellers' cheques are not accepted. Get your tax stamp signed before passport control.

Documents, see page 179.

Land borders
Kenya has land borders with Tanzania, Uganda, Sudan, Ethiopia and Somalia. All are officially open, but overland travel through southern Sudan and Somalia is highly inadvisable at present. If you are bringing in your own vehicle, you will need a Carnet (available through the AA) to avoid paying duty and you will need to buy local insurance on arrival in the first major town. An International Authorization Permit, issued free for the first seven days, is also required.

Arriving by sea
The Africa Shipping Corporation sometimes runs a catamaran service between Mombasa and Zanzibar (tel: 011-315 178). Ask local travel agents.

Sign language says it all

CAMPING

Kenya has raised camping to an art form, with every possible variation from a pup tent to a luxury permanent camp, where your tent comes with a bathroom. There are also plenty of independent campsites. Most are fairly basic, however, and you have to take in everything from firewood to drinking water. Camping outside the designated areas is highly inadvisable. One or two car hire companies will supply a safari vehicle complete with camping equipment, but it is almost as cheap, and much easier, to take one of the camping safaris offered by every tour operator in the country.

CHILDREN, see pages 158–9.

CLIMATE

Kenya is on the Equator but its altitudes and terrain vary enormously. Temperatures remain fairly stable all year round, as do the hours of daylight (roughly 6am to 6.30pm), but there are several distinct climatic regions.

The coast is always hot and humid, while the highlands are warm during the

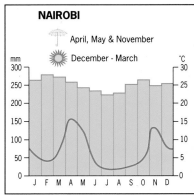

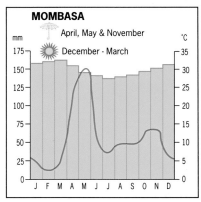

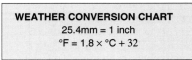

day and chilly at night. Western Kenya tends to be warm and relatively wet all year round, while the desert lands of the far north are always very hot and dry.

There are two rainy seasons, the short rains in October and November and the long rains from March to early June. There is a 'winter' in the highlands in

July and August, when the sky clouds over and the temperature drops slightly.

CONVERSION TABLES, see right.

CRIME, see **First Steps**, page 40.

TRAVELLERS WITH DISABILITIES
There are no special facilities for travellers with disabilities, but there is no shortage of goodwill or manpower. As long as you write ahead and tip generously, there will always be someone to help you. Stick to the more expensive hotels; facilities deteriorate once out of the 'tourist zone'. The public areas and some bedrooms at most resorts and game lodges are at ground level, while the larger Nairobi hotels have lifts. Few have special fittings or wide acess, however, so a travelling wheelchair is recommended. There are London taxis in Nairobi and Mombasa and, with a little juggling you can get a wheelchair into a safari minibus. For more information, contact the **Association for the Physically Disabled in Kenya**, *PO Box 46747, Nairobi (tel: 224443)*.

DOCUMENTS
All visitors must have a passport, with at least three months validity, and an onward ticket or proof of funds. Citizens of the UK, Canada, Ireland, Germany and Spain do not need visas; citizens of Australia, New Zealand, Holland, Italy, South Africa and the USA do. Other nationals should check with their local embassy. Allow plenty of time for applications as they can take 6 weeks.

Entry is normally for three months. Visa extensions are available from the Immigration Office, Nyayo House, corner Kenyatta Avenue/Uhuru Highway, Nairobi (tel: 332 110) or the Immigration Office, Mombasa (tel: 311 745).

Conversion Table

FROM	TO	MULTIPLY BY
Inches	Centimetres	2.54
Feet	Metres	0.3048
Yards	Metres	0.9144
Miles	Kilometres	1.6090
Acres	Hectares	0.4047
Gallons	Litres	4.5460
Ounces	Grams	28.35
Pounds	Grams	453.6
Pounds	Kilograms	0.4536
Tons	Tonnes	1.0160

To convert back, for example from centimetres to inches, divide by the number in the the third column.

Men's Suits

UK		36	38	40	42	44	46	48
Rest of Europe	46	48	50	52	54	56	58
US		36	38	40	42	44	46	48

Dress Sizes

UK		8	10	12	14	16	18
France		36	38	40	42	44	46
Italy		38	40	42	44	46	48
Rest of Europe	34	36	38	40	42	44
US		6	8	10	12	14	16

Men's Shirts

UK	14	14.5	15	15.5	16	16.5	17
Rest of Europe	36	37	38	39/40	41	42	43
US	14	14.5	15	15.5	16	16.5	17

Men's Shoes

UK		7	7.5	8.5	9.5	10.5	11
Rest of Europe	41	42	43	44	45	46
US		8	8.5	9.5	10.5	11.5	12

Women's Shoes

UK		4.5	5	5.5	6	6.5	7
Rest of Europe	38	38	39	39	40	41
US		6	6.5	7	7.5	8	8.5

ELECTRICITY

240 volts with three-square-pin plugs.
The power supply is generally reliable
although there are occasional failures and
some rationing due to excess demand or
storms. Most hotels and lodges have
their own generators, but a torch is
always useful and essential if camping.

EMBASSIES AND CONSULATES

Kenyan Embassies Worldwide

Australia
33–5 Ainslie Avenue, Canberra, ACT
2600 (tel: 247 4688).

Canada
Ste 600, 415 Laurier Avenue East, Ottawa
ON K1N 6R4 (tel: 613-563 1773).

UK
45 Portland Place, London W1N 4AS
(tel: 0171-636 2371).

USA
2249 R St NW, Washington DC 20008
(tel: 440 215).
866 United Nations Plaza, New York
NY 10017 (tel: 421 4740).

Foreign Embassies in Nairobi

Australia
New Chancery, Riverside Drive (PO Box
39341), (tel: 445 034).

Canada
Comcraft House, Haile Selassie Avenue
(PO Box 30481), (tel: 214 804; fax: 226
987).

Ireland
O'Washika Road, Lavington (PO Box
30659), (tel: 562 615; fax: 540 048).

UK
Bruce House, Standard Street (PO Box
30465), (tel: 335 944/60).

USA
Embassy Building, Moi Avenue (PO Box
30137), (tel: 334 141/50).
For other countries, see the phone
directory or *What's On*.

EMERGENCY TELEPHONE NUMBERS

Dial 999 and ask for police, fire or
ambulance.
MasterCard card loss or theft: 000 1 314
542 7111 (call collect).
Thomas Cook Travellers' Cheques loss
or theft: 000 44 1733 318950 (call
collect). The Thomas Cook Network
locations listed on pages 188–9 will
provide emergency assistance in cases of
loss or theft of MasterCards or Thomas
Cook Travellers' Cheques.

GETTING AROUND

By air

There is a wide network of domestic
flights operating from Moi International in
Mombasa (see page 177) and Wilson
Airport, Nairobi. Malindi and Kisumu
also have small airports and most other
towns and major game parks have air
strips. Most tour operators offer flying
options. Tickets prices are very reasonable
and if you are in a group, it will cost little
more to charter the plane yourself.

Wilson Airport
Langata Road (PO Box 19011), Nairobi
(tel: 501 941). 5km south of the city
centre.
Moi International, see page 177.
Kisumu Airport
Nyerere Road (PO Box 12), Kisumu
(tel: 40125).
Malindi Airport
Mombasa Road (PO Box 67), Malindi
(tel: 20981).

Kenya Airways (see page 176) is the
main, state-run domestic carrier.
Air Kenya, Wilson Airport (PO Box
30357), Nairobi (tel: 501 601/2/3/4).
Regular services from Nairobi to
Mombasa, Kisumu and Malindi.

The main private air carriers include **Eagle Aviation** (Mombasa to Lamu), **Prestige Air Services**, and **Skyways Airlines**. Book through a travel agent who will be able to find the most convenient and cheapest deal.

By rail, see page 146. The Thomas Cook Overseas Timetable, published monthly, gives rail schedules for Kenya.

By road
Car hire

Car hire is very expensive. If you are planning any touring, a four-wheel-drive vehicle is advisable and often essential. The unlimited mileage deals are cheapest, but also look at chauffeur-driven options. It is little more expensive as you will not have to pay the crippling insurance and CDW. Your driver will know how to tackle the appalling roads, steer you away from conmen who target foreign motorists and will also be an excellent tour guide. There are many car hire firms in Nairobi and Mombasa, but virtually none elsewhere. Listed are the most reliable.

Avis

2nd Floor, College House, Nairobi (tel: 336 703); fax: 215 421); Jomo Kenyatta International Airport (tel: 822 186); Moi Avenue, Mombasa (book via Nairobi office).

Concorde Car Hire

Agip Petrol Station, Waiyaki Way, Westlands (PO Box 25053), Nairobi (tel: 448 953 or fax: 448 135); and Meru Road (PO Box 831 183), Mombasa (tel: 223 502 or fax: 228 162).

Hertz

This is the local giant, operated by UTC (see page 189 for main addresses). There are also offices in Malindi (tel: 0123-20069) and Diani (tel: 0127-2149), with desks at Moi and JKI airports, and the main hotels in Nairobi and Mombasa.

Southern Cross Safaris

Standard Street, New Stanley Hotel (PO Box 56707), Nairobi (tel: 225 255 or fax: 216 553); and Ambalal House, Nkrumah Road (PO Box 99456), Mombasa (tel: 229 520/1/2/3/4/5/6 or fax: 314 226).

Driving

Driving is on the left, giving way to traffic coming in from the right at intersections. Your national licence is valid for 90 days, but an international one would be better. Fuel is available in all towns and at most game lodges, but it is advisable to carry a jerry can if heading out of town. Try to be off the road by dark, both for security and because of the many lethal vehicles with no lights.

With the exception of a few major toll-roads around Nairobi and Mombasa, the quality of the roads varies from poor to diabolical. Journeys are usually much slower and more tiring than you would expect, and you will almost inevitably have to cope with breakdowns, punctures and even getting stuck. Make sure you have a good set of tools, a good spare tyre and preferably a new inner tube as well. The locals are usually helpful, for a price, and there is someone in every village to mend the punctures. On isolated roads or in the parks, report in to the ranger or police station so that someone knows where you are.

Hitch-hiking

Do not hitch. It is possible, but is very dangerous these days. The best way to find a lift is to ask around the hotels and campsites. Expect to split petrol costs.

Public Transport, see page 188.

Multi-lingual AIDS warning – part of the government's health education campaign

HEALTH

AIDS

Aids is endemic in Kenya with 750,000 people officially HIV positive and estimates of as many as 28 per cent infected between the ages of 20 and 40. This is no reason to be alarmed as you will only be at risk if you sleep around. Avoid the temptations of the huge numbers of prostitutes, and always use a condom. Take a pack of sterile needles (available from any good pharmacy) and insist on using them if you need an injection. If you need a blood transfusion, throw yourself on the mercy of your friends or contact your embassy. Some have lists of 'clean' donors and even blood banks.

Altitude sickness

This is only a problem on high altitude hikes, such as the trek up Mount Kenya. See pages 76–7.

Bilharzia

This small, unpleasant worm uses freshwater snails as its intermediate host. You should be safe in very cold or fast-flowing water, but to be safe, stay out of all fresh water except swimming pools. If you do get wet, towel off briskly within a few minutes. If you feel you have been at risk, get a simple test done at your nearest tropical diseases unit. Treatment is easy if the disease is caught in time.

Cuts and scratches

These minor scrapes can easily become infected, septic and even ulcerous in the tropics. Clean them out thoroughly, apply anti-septic and keep them covered up. If you see signs of infection, take antibiotics.

Inoculations

Yellow fever is mandatory if travelling from an infected area and advisable anyway. Also recommended: typhoid, polio, tetanus and hepatitis A. Allow two months for a full set.

Hospitals and doctors

For routine treatments, the quality of healthcare is good. Most doctors have trained, or spent some time working in the West, and you may well be treated by a Western aid worker. All staff speak English and you can usually find someone who speaks French, German or Italian. For anything more complicated, the best hospitals in the country are:

Nairobi Hospital, Argwings Kodhek Road, Nairobi (tel: 723 017/722 160/720 624).

The Aga Khan Hospital, 3rd Avenue, Parklands, Nairobi (tel: 742 531/747 676).

The Aga Khan Hospital, Nyerere Road, Mombasa (tel: 312 953/4/5).

There are numerous other hospitals listed in *What's On* magazine. Private clinics are generally better stocked with drugs and equipment and will be more comfortable if you have to stay in. Make sure your travel insurance will cover the costs and, if necessary, will cover a medivac flight home.

Many rural hospitals are basic clinics. If in doubt, contact the local mission. If planning to stray off the beaten track, take out temporary membership of the Amref Flying Doctor Service, Wilson Airport, PO Box 30125, Nairobi (tel: 501301/500508; telex: 23254 AMREF; fax: 506112; or Africa Air Rescue (K) Ltd, Kenyatta Avenue, P O Box 41766 (tel: 337 504/337 030).

Malaria

Malaria can be a killer. Prescribed dosages of anti-malarial prophylactics must be taken for two weeks before arrival, during your stay, and continued for two weeks after departure. Use repellents and mosquito nets to avoid being bitten. The disease is carried only by the female anopheles mosquito, which comes out at night. Local malaria has developed immunity to the most common anti-malarial drug, chloroquine, so it should be taken alongside one of the other drugs, or replaced by one of the newer substitutes. Get up-to-date advice from a specialist travel clinic or malaria hotline. If you show flu-like symptoms at any time, up to six months after your return home, ask your GP for a malaria test.

Stomach bugs

Kenya is a pretty hygienic place and there is little likelihood of getting a bug. Wash your hands before touching food, do not eat in obviously dirty establishments, or touch food that has been left lying around. If in doubt, drink bottled mineral water, and ask for drinks without ice. If you do get caught, try and sweat it out for 24 hours, eating nothing and drinking lots, particularly drinks with salt and sugar in them. The chief danger is from dehydration. If you need to keep on the move, the most effective 'concrete' is immodium. If it lasts more than 48 hours, consult a doctor.

Sunburn and heatstroke

There is a huge temptation to spend every daylight hour on the beach or, in the cooler highlands, to forget you are on the Equator. The sun here is fierce. Always wear a hat, don't spend too long out in any one sitting, and use a high-factor sunblock. If you do get burned, use huge amounts of aftersun cream. Heatstroke occurs when the body's cooling system is strained so far that it breaks down, causing the body temperature to rise uncontrollably. If this happens, get the sufferer into a cold bath immediately and call for medical help.

Rabies

Unless you are planning to handle animals, an inoculation against rabies should be unnecessary. Should you have the misfortune to be bitten, however, you must start a course of treatment immediately. If you wait for symptoms to appear, it is too late.

INSURANCE

Good travel insurance is highly advisable. Most importantly, you should have good, all-purpose medical cover, including medivac facilities. In addition, it should cover third-party liability, legal assistance, loss of personal possessions (including cash, travellers' cheques and documents) and should contain some facility for cancellation and delay in your travel arrangements. If you are planning to take part in any adventure sports, check that your policy will cover you (most won't), and, if necessary, get an extension. Travel insurance does not normally cover you for liability arising from motor accidents; this requires an extra top-up policy.

LANGUAGE

See opposite.

LOST PROPERTY

The hotels usually have a lost property department, but there are no official facilities in the country at large. Try the police or contact *The Nation* newspaper who run a finding service through their Sunday edition. Your chances of recovering your possessions are pretty slim.

MAPS

Bartholomews, Macmillan and Nelles all do good country maps for Kenya. There is an excellent 1:50,000 annotated map of Mount Kenya by A Wielochowski and M Savage. These are all available in good bookshops, both in Kenya and abroad. Other than that, most local maps tend to be elderly and out of date and, therefore, you would do better to stick to the maps in this book.

MEDIA

There are three English language daily newspapers, *The Nation*, *The Kenya Times* and *The Standard*. The biggest and most useful is *The Nation*. A wide range of foreign papers is available a few days late in Nairobi and Mombasa. The main English language radio station and the single nationwide TV station are both run by the government-owned Kenya Broadcasting Corporation. Within a 40km radius of Nairobi, there is a second, far better TV channel partly owned by CNN.

Headquarters of *The Nation* media group, Nairobi

LANGUAGE

Each of Kenya's many tribes has its own language but Swahili is the official language of government. Strictly speaking, it is Kiswahili that is used. This is the inland dialect of the original language and, although they can understand it easily enough, the Swahili people of the coast pour scorn on what they see as a bastard off-shoot.

You will almost always find someone who speaks English and if you don't, chances are you are in a remote tribal location with people who can't speak Swahili either! On the coast, most resorts will have German and Italian speakers on the staff, and there will usually be someone near by with at least a smattering of French or Spanish. Inland, you are less likely to find such a range.

Survival is easy, but it is considered good manners to learn at least a few words of greeting in Swahili, and can add to the enjoyment of your holiday. The language is written phonetically, so the most obvious pronunciation is correct. There are plenty of good phrase books and language tapes for those who wish to learn more.

Useful Swahili words

Welcome	**Karibu**
Hello	**Jambo**
How are you?	**Habari?**
Very well	**Mzuri sana**
Goodbye	**Kwaheri/**
(plural)	**Kwaherini**
Please	**Tafhadali**
Thank you	**Asante**
Thank you very much	**Asante sana**
Yes	**Ndiyo**
No	**Hapana**
Sir	**Bwana**
Madam	**Mama**
OK	**Sawa sawa**
I don't understand	**Sielewi**
Do you speak English?	**Unasema Kingereza?**
Excuse me	**Samahani**
No problem	**Hakuna matata**
Food	**Chakula**
Doctor	**Daktari**
How much?	**Bei gani?**
Money	**Pesa**

Glossary of Common Terms

Soldier/watchman	**Askari**
Small dwelling	**Banda**
Village	**Boma**
Tea	**Chai**
Small shop	**Duka**
Village	**Manyatta**
Passenger vehicle	**Matatu**
Tribal warrior(s)	**Moran/Murani**
Dirt road	**Murram**
White person	**Mzungu**
Roast meat	**Nyama choma**
Maize meal	**Posho**
Any journey	**Safari**
Smallholding	**Shamba**

Most signs are in English and Swahili

POSSESSION OF A PLATFORM TICKET DOES NOT ENTITLE THE HOLDER TO BOARD A TRAIN.

TIKITI YA KUINGIA STESHENI HAIMRUHUSU MTU KUINGIA GARINI

PLATFORM TICKETS

MONEY MATTERS

Currency
The unit of currency is the Kenya shilling, divided into 100 cents. There are 10, 20, 50, 100, 200 and 500 shilling notes; and 5, 10 and 50 cent, and 1 and 5 shilling coins. It can be difficult to change large denomination notes. For import restrictions, see Customs on page 177.

Exchange facilities
Most banks in Nairobi and Mombasa, and at least one in the smaller towns, will handle foreign exchange. Rates are standard, but the commission varies, as does the amount of red tape. Probably the easiest bank to use is Barclays.

Banking hours are usually Monday to Friday, 9am to 2pm, and on the first and last Saturday of each month, 9am to 11am. The Nairobi International and Mombasa airport exchange desks are open 24 hours a day.

Most tourist hotels and lodges will also exchange money for their guests, although some of the smaller ones may well have an upper limit of around US$100.

Cheques and credit cards
Thomas Cook Travellers' Cheques are readily accepted; they should preferably be denominated in US dollars, as these are easiest to use.

Credit cards are accepted by all good hotels, and most up-market restaurants and shops. The most widely recognised are Visa, MasterCard and Barclaycard. Some shops add a small surcharge for credit card sales.

Prices
A few years ago, the Kenyan government introduced separate non-resident rates, to be paid in hard currency, for all good hotels and organised safaris. Most companies took the opportunity to raise their prices dramatically. At the same time, a two-tier system was set up for museums and game parks. Most museums now charge foreigners double, and at the time of writing, game park fees are nine times higher for non-residents. Once outside this system, and with the exception of car hire, Kenya is pretty cheap.

NATIONAL HOLIDAYS

1 January: New Year's Day
March/April: Good Friday, Easter Monday
1 May: Labour Day
1 June: Madaraka Day (anniversary of self-government)
10 October: Moi Day (anniversary of Moi's inauguration)
20 October: Kenyatta Day (anniversary of Kenyatta's arrest)
12 December: Jamhuri Day (anniversary of independence)
25 December: Christmas Day
26 December: Boxing Day
Idd-ul-Fitr: Muslim celebration of the end of Ramadan (variable from year to year)

NATIONAL PARKS
Kenya has over 40 national parks, covering in all an area larger than Switzerland. Although some are run by the local council; the vast majority, including the coastal marine parks, come under the auspices of the Kenya Wildlife Services.

All parks are open from 6am to 6pm and you must be either out of the park or in camp by curfew. Only a few (those without large predators) will allow you in on foot, and in all parks your vehicle must be registered in Kenya.

OPENING HOURS

Listed under the relevant sections throughout this book.

PHARMACIES

There are numerous pharmacies in Nairobi and Mombasa, and at least one in each small town. Many open from 8am to 8pm and at least one will stay open late each evening. The roster or an out of hours contact number should be posted in the window and is published in *The Nation* newspaper and *What's On* magazine.

PLACES OF WORSHIP

Kenya is literally teeming with churches which cover every conceivable denomination. The larger towns also have at least one Hindu temple and one mosque, while on the predominantly Muslim coast, the various branches of Islam are all represented. There is a Jewish Synagogue in Nairobi.

POLICE

The huge numbers of police roadblocks are officially there to check vehicles, but most are actually there for the bribes. Sadly the police force in Kenya is riddled with corruption. A 'white' car is rarely stopped and will never be tapped for cash. If you run into trouble, you should be treated with courtesy, but take someone with you as a precaution. If you are arrested, you could be in for a very rough time, so make sure that someone gets word to the embassy or a lawyer as soon as possible. As a rule always be polite to the police and never take photographs.

The Swaminarayan Hindu Temple Mombasa

POST

The postal system, although fairly reliable, is somewhat sluggish. It is important to remember that when sending parcels, you must take them in unwrapped for inspection by Customs. All post offices have *poste restante* facilities, but the pigeon-holing can be eccentric, so make sure that your correspondents write clearly and underline your surname. Post offices are open Monday to Friday, 8am to 5pm; and on Saturdays, 8am to 1pm.

PUBLIC TRANSPORT
Buses
There are plenty of tatty buses operating in the main cities, but relatively few long-distance ones. Prices are cheap, but most are very uncomfortable and overcrowded.

Matatus
These brightly painted vans are a cross between a bus and shared taxi. Found everywhere they are cheap, useful, uncomfortable, crowded and dangerous, accounting for most road deaths.

Taxis
There are taxis outside the main hotels and on main streets. Negotiate a price before you get in. Taxis are not cheap.

SENIOR CITIZENS
There are no special facilities or discounts for the elderly, but few tours involve a lot of walking, the facilities are comfortable, and the range of food wide. The elderly should have no problems.

London taxis are an increasingly common sight in the streets of Nairobi and Mombasa

STUDENT AND YOUTH TRAVEL
The YHA and YMCA have Kenyan bases (see page 171), otherwise, there are no special facilities or discounts for young travellers. TST Tours, PO Box 50982, Nairobi (tel: 791 227 or fax: 780 461) specialise in technical or study tours in a wide range of fields for students and professionals on working trips.

TELEPHONES
The domestic and international phone systems both work efficiently and most places are on the STD network for direct dialling. The hotels all charge high premiums, so try and use an outside phone. The streets of Nairobi are littered with phone boxes, but not all have phones in them yet. The international dialling code for Kenya is 254.

Operator: 900
Directory enquiries: 991
International STD: 000 or 001
International operator: 0196
International information and call booking: 0191

Telex and fax
Most businesses and hotels have both fax and telex facilities, but they don't come cheap. There are public phones and faxes suitable for international calls in the Extelcom building in Nairobi (Haile Selassie Avenue; open 8am to midnight), the Kenyatta International Conference Centre (City Square), and the main post office in Mombasa (Nyerere Avenue).

THOMAS COOK
The Thomas Cook Worldwide Network licensee is **UTC**, the most experienced tour operator in Kenya. UTC arranges tours, group travel and Hertz car hire, and provides emergency assistance to MasterCard cardholders and Thomas

Cook Travellers' Cheques holders. Addresses are as follows:

Nairobi: Fedha Towers, Muindi Mbingu Street, PO Box 42196 (tel: 331 960 or fax: 216 871).

Mombasa: Moi Avenue, PO Box 84782 (tel: 316 333/4 or fax: 314 549).

Malindi: PO Box 365 (tel: 20040/20069 or fax: 30443).

TIME

GMT +3. When it is noon in Kenya, it is 9am in London, 4am in New York, 1am on the West Coast of America, and 7pm in Sydney, Australia.

TIPPING

There is usually a 10 per cent service charge built into hotel and restaurant bills, so tipping is an optional extra. A small amount will do for bags or other services and tipping is unnecessary in bars or taxis. At the end of a safari leave the staff a decent tip or present.

TOILETS

Avoid public toilets; use those in the hotels and restaurants. Those in good establishments are excellent; in the very cheap ones, roll up your trousers and hold your nose. Campsite toilets are usually clean and hygienic long-drops, but look out for other inhabitants – from cockroaches to bats! If camping in the bush, bury or burn your paper. Always carry some paper or tissues.

TOURIST OFFICES
Tourist Offices Abroad
UK

25 Brooks Mews, London W1Y 1LG (tel: 0171-355 3144).

USA

424 Madison Avenue, New York NY 10017 (tel: 212/486 1300 or fax:

212/688 0911); and 9150 Wilshire Boulevard, Ste 60, Beverly Hills CA 90121 (tel: 310/274 6635 or fax: 310/859 7010). There are also offices in Frankfurt, Paris, Zurich, and Stockholm. In Kenya, there are relatively useless offices in Moi Avenue, Mombasa (tel: 311 231), and in Utali House, Utali Street, opposite Uhuru Highway, Nairobi (tel: 331030).

TOUR OPERATORS AND AGENTS

There are some 600 tour operators in Kenya. To obtain a comprehensive list, contact the **Kenya Association of Tour Operators** (**KATO**), Jubilee Insurance Exchange Building, Mama Ngina Street (PO Box 48461), Nairobi (tel: 225 570; fax: 218 402). For more specialist operators, see page 143.

Bush Homes

Small company handling home stays on private ranches and walking safaris. Wilson Airport (PO Box 56923), Nairobi (tel: 502 491/506 139 or fax: 502 739).

Let's Go Travel Ltd

Popular with local expats, LGT will arrange anything and everything. Offices also in Karen and Westlands. Caxton House, Standard Street, PO Box 60342, Nairobi (tel: 340 331/213 033 or fax: 336 890).

Southern Cross Safaris

Central booking for air travel, car hire, tours and safaris, hotels and lodges. (See page 181 for details.)

UTC

The giant of Kenyan tourism. The Thomas Cook Network licensee in Kenya (see **Thomas Cook** above), UTC also handles Block Hotels, Hertz Cars and a wide range of tours and safaris to most destinations at all prices, except rock-bottom.

ACKNOWLEDGEMENTS

The Automobile Association wishes to thank the following organisations, libraries and photographers for their assistance in the preparation of this book.

ARDEA LONDON 113a (L & T. Bomford), 113b (J Mackinnon)
CAMERAPIX 128
THE HULTON DEUTSCH COLLECTION 145
THE ILLUSTRATED LONDON NEWS 66
IMPACT PHOTOS 19a (J Stjerneklar)
PAUL KENWARD 133, 136a, 136b, 158
MARY EVANS PICTURE LIBRARY 28b
NATURE PHOTOGRAPHERS LTD 6 (D Hutton), 19b (R Tidman), 25a (P R Sterry), 32 (D Hutton), 41 (S C Bisserot), 85b (R S Daniell), 89 (B Burbidge), 135b (R Tidman), 137 (P R Sterry), 143 (M Gore)
MELISSA SHALES 5, 16, 19c, 29b, 62, 72, 81, 96, 97, 118, 119, 121, 138b, 139, 142, 151
SPECTRUM COLOUR LIBRARY 76, 78, 79, 116
TOPHAM PICTURE SOURCE 29a (Associated Press), 106a
TRUSTEES OF THE BRITISH MUSEUM 135a
ZEFA PICTURE LIBRARY (UK) LTD

The remaining photographs are held in the AA Photo Library and were taken by Paul Kenward, with the exception of pages 1, 11, 20, 28a, 55, 66/7, 67, 75a, 75b, 94, 104, 117, 126, 127, 146a, 150, 152, 165, 166a, 167, 173, 185, 188 which were taken by Eric Meacher.

The Automobile Association would also like to thank Carl Ogola of Thomas Cook Ltd, Nairobi, and Mr D N Njoroge, Director General of the Automobile Association of Kenya, for their assistance during the preparation of this book.

The author would like to thank the following people and companies for their invaluable assistance: John Glenn, Liz Mbogori, John Lyall, Will and Emma Craig, Tony and Adrienne Mills, Clement Mwatsama and Malcolm Gascoigne; UTC, Yare Safaris, Bookings Ltd, Kenya Airways, Lonrho Hotels, African Safari Club, Alliance Hotels, Concorde Car Hire, Sarova Hotels, and Windsor Hotels in Kenya, and Safari Consultants, Skyway to Africa and Wildlife Safari in the UK.

CONTRIBUTORS

Series adviser: Melissa Shales
Thanks also to Melissa Shales for her updating work on this revised edition